Anti-Bride Guide

Anti-Bride Guide

TYING THE KNOT OUTSIDE OF THE BOX

by Carolyn Gerin and Stephanie Rosenbaum

CHRONICLE BOOKS
SAN FRANCISCO

Library of Congress Cataloging-in-Publication Data:
Gerin, Carolyn.
Anti-bride guide: tying the knot outside of the box
by Carolyn Gerin and Stephanie Rosenbaum.
p. cm.
ISBN 0-8118-2967-7
1. Weddings—Planning. I. Rosenbaum, Stephanie. II. Title.
HQ745 .G47 2001
395.2'2—dc21
2001017082

Printed in China
Art Direction: Carolyn Gerin, Subset Design
Design: Carolyn Gerin, Ithinand Tubkam, Subset Design
Illustrations: Ithinand Tubkam
Illustration Assistance: Gregory Nersesian
Production: Bert W. Green, Circle Elephant Art

Distributed in Canada by Raincoast Books
9050 Shaughnessy Street
Vancouver, British Columbia V6P 6E5

10 9 8 7 6 5

Chronicle Books LLC
85 Second Street
San Francisco, California 94105

www.chroniclebooks.com

CONTENTS

Growing up in suburbia in the 1970s, my sisters and I were enthralled by one particular board game. While Gloria Steinem, Billie Jean King, and Betty Friedan were doing their best to get women out of the kitchen and into the streets, we couldn't wait to plunk down on the three-tone shag carpet and lift the lid of a big pink box embossed with "The Bride Game" in frilly white script. Unlike Risk or Monopoly, there wasn't much substance to The Bride Game. Competition, and even winning, weren't the point. Instead, it was a romantic consumerist fantasy: build a bridal identity based on *stuff*. You rolled a pair of dice to become one of four brides—spring, summer, autumn, winter—with accompanying grooms and bridesmaids. Then, the only goal was to accumulate the required pile of gear—cake, ring, bouquet, something borrowed, something blue—as you moved down the hot-pink steps toward the altar.

Of course, it's almost impossible to imagine any toy company blithely selling such a game today. Or is it? From honeymoon cruises to plastic cake toppers, Americans shell out roughly $45 billion a year for weddings. With an average of 2.5 million couples tying the knot in a given year, that's about $15,000 per wedding. Of course, some weddings are as simple as a backyard potluck; others (the kind involving orchids flown in from Thailand and taking place on private islands) can stretch to six figures. Stuffed with advertisements, the average bridal magazine makes even the big, juicy September issue of *Vogue* look puny by comparison. For most first-time brides, the real problem with planning a wedding is getting deluged with too many "shoulds."

We've watched a lot of otherwise smart, sassy brides-to-be drive themselves crazy trying to make everyone happy. The first accessory we recommend for any anti-bride is a pair of earplugs—not real ones, but rather some big, fluffy, imaginary earmuffs that float snugly around your head every time your future mother-in-law, your coworker, or your florist starts telling you what you must, should, or ought to do at your wedding. Because you know what? It's all up to you and your partner. Yes, there are tons of traditions, some cultural, some religious, and some just traditional. But regardless of what your mom (or Emily Post) implies, your marriage will not disintegrate if you don't send every guest home with a little box of color-coordinated Jordan almonds inscribed with your names in fancy script. While we were putting together this book, we asked dozens of couples how they got hitched. The last question we asked every bride was, "What was the coolest part of your wedding?" Not one mentioned the miniature quiches or the great deal she got on her Vera Wang gown. Instead, they told us about "the enormous numbers of friends who came from far and wide" and "the toasts given by our friends that went on longer and were much more heartfelt than expected." One bride shared the moment of "hearing my husband-to-be say 'I do,' and looking into his beautiful, dark eyes and seeing the truth: love, eternity, and devotion." For another bride, after the ceremony, the cake, and the final departure of the last guest, it was all about "finally being alone with my fella—and going on a Fritos binge!"

After all, if all you cared about was having the most perfect wedding cake in the universe, you'd be reading *Martha Stewart Weddings* instead, right?

That's not to say you should give up being a princess. At what other time do you get to plan, stage-manage, and then (wearing a really fabulous outfit) star in your very own show? After all, we love pedicures, presents, and Champagne as much as the next girl (if not more). And unless you're Miss America or Madonna, you'll probably never have so many people dedicated to making you beautiful as you will for this one day.

That's where the concept of the *anti-bride* comes in. When we first started working on this book, some of our friends didn't get it right away. What was *with* the title? How could we be writing a wedding guide without a bride in it? Did we think everyone should just get hitched at City Hall on their lunch hour, with no veil, no cake, no bouquet? This led to a lot of Merlot-fueled musings on just what being a bride was all about. Could a girl be a hip, independent woman, able to fix her own carburetor and hook up her own hard drive, but still harbor a deep craving for matching china and fancy matchbooks?

Well, of course! An anti-bride is a bride who's getting married her own way. In fact, we'd met a lot of anti-brides before we even began this book. As bridesmaids, sisters, roommates, and friends, we'd spent hours hanging out with a lot of really awesome about-to-be or recently married women who were thrilled to be hooking up with their sweethearts—but more than a little weirded out by the weight of the myriad monogrammed-and-engraved traditions they were suddenly expected to take on. While we all shared the same image of the bride as a blushing young woman floating down the aisle frosted head-to-toe in white satin and lace, the reality couldn't have been more different. You're not living the same kind of life your mother or grandmother had. Why should you get married the same way? None of the brides we knew wanted anyone—much less the wedding industry—to dictate what kind of bride she should be. At the same time, we still crave ceremony, ritual, and, yes, a fabulous dress to mark this momentous occasion. The anti-bride is proud to be getting married, but she isn't just anyone's—or any magazine's—bride. She is her own bride, making it up as she goes along, creating her own traditions, and picking and choosing what's right for her and for her partner, without losing her identity along the way. And, like so many of us, she doesn't like being told what to do, especially if it involves wearing ugly white shoes.

Maybe, as an anti-bride yourself, you'll wear white and arrive at your wedding in a horse-drawn carriage. Maybe you'll buzz in on the back of your fiancé's (or your own) Harley. Maybe you'll walk down the aisle by yourself. Maybe you'll be holding a bouquet, or carrying a baby, or just hanging on tightly to your fiancé's hand. Maybe you'll be making your lifetime commitment to another woman. Just by virtue of getting married, you'll be a bride. And that means any outfit you wear that day counts as a wedding dress, and any party you hold is a wedding reception. To us, an anti-bride is a cool chick who gets to have (and eat) her cake, work her style to the max, and dance the night away. After all, what's the point of having a wedding if you don't get to dance?

Naturally, it's one thing to make grand pronouncements of freedom and independence when the big day is still eight months off. It's quite another to be standing there shivering in your underwear as two determined saleswomen tug a huge cupcake of tulle down over your hips. The *Anti-Bride Guide* is set up to steer you as painlessly as possible through the process of creating your wedding—and to be a little voice of sanity that will get you through even the most trying days lurking ahead. First, grab a pencil and skim through Chapter 1, "Getting Started." Here, you'll find a handy questionnaire that will help you figure out just what kind of event you want. Somewhere between the wedding you've dreamed about and the wedding you can afford, you'll find the perfect fit for you and your partner. Formal or casual? On the beach or inside a gallery? With all the pals on your e-mail list, or just your closest friends and family? Once you've got the basic style and size settled, move on to Chapter 2, "Places and Spaces." Who says a wedding has to take place in a designated "wedding" space? We don't see any reason to settle for polyester tablecloths in a generic hotel ballroom when for the same price (or a lot less!) you could hold your wedding in one of many beautiful and offbeat locations. We've dug up dozens of location ideas for memorable ceremonies and receptions, from ski lodges to barns. Pick your place, and then it's on to Chapter 3, "Ambiance," for invitations (not necessarily on engraved cream-colored stationery), fabulous centerpieces, bountiful buffets, and music that will have your guests dancing 'til the sun comes up.

Chapter 4, "The Ceremony," comes next, with special attention given to writing your own vows, shopping around for an officiant, and deciding how to get friends and family involved. This is, of course, the most serious part of the whole project, so we won't blame you if you flip ahead to Chapter 5, "The Dress"! Learn to "speak gown," find bridesmaids' dresses that make everyone look good (yes, it *can* be done), and find out what to ask for—and avoid—when you're shopping. You'll find it all here, plus dozens of ways to update a vintage gown or go retro with class. And whether you're looking for a barrette or a tiara, platform shoes or feathered mules, Chapter 6, "Accessories," is jammed with advice from stylists, designers, and all-around groovy gals on how to make your outfit look like a million bucks (it all starts with beads and a glue gun!). Finally, Chapter 7, "The Main Event," will help you stay stress free on the big day, with loads of advice on making time for your girlfriends, your sweetie, and your adoring public.

The most important thing you can do is relax and enjoy your life *now*. In the midst of planning this big event, it's easy to lose sight of the reason for all the froufrou: You're in love! After all the flakes, the weirdos, and the hotties who never called back, you've finally discovered Mr. Wonderful. For the rest of your life (we hope), you'll have a lover, a best friend, a sweetheart to kiss every New Year's Eve, and, what's most important, someone to squash that scary spider in the bathroom for you, even in the middle of the night. While you're planning your wedding, don't let your partner get shoved offstage and, more importantly, don't assume you can just stick your relationship in the fridge for six months while you run from cake tastings to bridal salons.

A wedding is not an end in itself. Yes, as rituals go, it is a big deal. But it's also the very beginning of your marriage. There are many steps to take down the road, and lots of issues to be decided that will ultimately be far more important than your wedding tablecloth colors, or even the bandleader knocking back three tequila sunrises and hitting on your mom during the reception.

Our best advice? Do what you want, don't let anyone else stress you out, and have fun!

Note: For simplicity's sake, we've used the terms "groom," "fiancé," and "boyfriend" throughout the book. However, we hope that everyone can use and enjoy The *Anti-Bride Guide* and we specifically wrote this book for any and all couples wishing to affirm their love and commitment to one another.

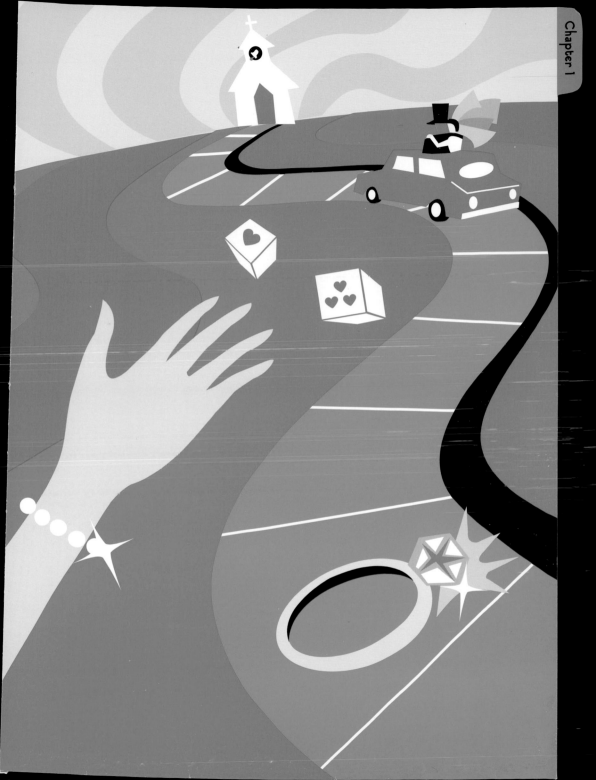

Getting Started: Fantasy to Reality

SELECTING A DATE

Most of the wedding guides we've seen assume you'll get engaged at least a year before your wedding date and that you'll happily spend every spare minute of those twelve months interviewing caterers and going to bridal salons. Yikes. What about going on dates? Or road trips? What about writing, painting, reading, playing music, and taking the dog out? It's easy to forget about the rest of your life when you get obsessed. We say, if you're going to be obsessed, find a topic that's more lasting than getting your bridesmaids' dresses to match the mint baskets.

Who knows, maybe a year ago you were totally single. Maybe you were dating your now-fiancé's then-roommate. Maybe you used to have a girlfriend, but situations changed and now you've got not just a boyfriend but an almost-husband. Maybe love didn't bloom—or the Vegas chapel didn't beckon—until just a few weeks or months ago. Well, relax. You can put together a wedding any way you want to. You may have already narrowed it down, roughly, to a time of year, a locale (or at least a type of locale), and a few must-have elements. Before you start making phone calls, think about how much you can (or would like to) devote to putting this show together. Both long- and short-term planning have their benefits.

Long-Term Planning (eight months or more)

Benefits
- Lots of options. You'll be more likely to get the time and place you want if you call to reserve early. This is especially true for popular locations, caterers, florists, etc., during the prime time (i.e., April through June, Christmas, and Valentine's Day) slots.
- Low-stress planning. Because there's no rush, you can do a little at a time, with plenty of time left over for your real life.
- Getting in sync with your partner. The longer you plan together, the more you can discover how your styles mesh.

Drawbacks

- Detail mania. The more time you have available, the more time you might spend sweating over every tiny item.
- Cash drain. Lots of cash tied up for months in 50-percent security deposits.
- The gossip grapevine. Lots of time for all those former coworkers and second cousins to hear about the wedding and assume they're invited.
- The family grapevine. Plenty of time for all those family members (yours or your fiancé's) to hear about the wedding and assume you want—or need—their advice.

Short-Term Planning (four months or less)

Benefits

- Originality. Necessity is the mother of invention, and this is never truer than with quickie wedding planning. You'll have to get creative, especially with regard to location. Often, you'll discover much more affordable and intriguing solutions, since the plan-ahead girls will have already booked all the obvious places.
- Less stress. A "let's-get-married-next-month" wedding is often a smaller, more intimate event. You get your favorite people together, pledge your troth, have a party, and go home.

Drawbacks

- Last-minute airline fares. They hurt. At least try to give your out-of-town guests enough notice to take advantage of thirty-day advance fares. The same goes for honeymoon plans. That dream week in Barbados could become a weekend camping in the Catskills when you find out what those will cost you.
- More stress. A lot of people will be happy to tell you that you *can't* plan a wedding in less than a year, and it's easy to short-circuit yourself trying to squeeze a lot of details into a few weeks.
- Extra legwork. Depending on where you live, your options for great cake bakers, florists, hair stylists, etc., may be limited, which means

you may spend a lot more time getting referrals and trying to track down someone to make your cake, bouquet, or tiara.

- Rush fees. What you don't put down in deposits, you can end up paying in rush charges, whether to get the seamstress to finish your dress on time or to have your bridesmaids' gifts delivered by overnight mail.

If you've got the luxury of planning your wedding anytime during the upcoming year, start by choosing your season. As you can probably guess, spring and summer are the busiest seasons for the wedding industry. Things slow down in winter and early spring, with the exception of the Christmas, New Year, and Valentine's Day holidays. Planning your wedding around a three-day weekend like Labor Day or Memorial Day may seem like a great idea, but if that's your goal, be sure to nail down your location (and nearby accommodations for yourself and your guests) as far in advance as possible, especially if you're aiming for a popular summer resort area. Be aware of dates that might cause conflicts for some of your guests. Planning a wedding for Arbor Day shouldn't offend anyone, but do check to make sure that your wedding doesn't fall on any religious holiday (like Yom Kippur or Good Friday) that would take precedence for devout guests.

> **TIP:** *Tampon absorbency: it's not what you want to be worrying about on your wedding day. Who wants to walk down the aisle wondering if that super-plus is up to the job? If possible, plan so that your period (and your PMS) is out of the way at least a week before the wedding.*

A bride who planned her whole wedding in less than a month admits it was hectic, but she points out that "the farther out you plan, the more people you have to invite and the more input everyone thinks they have." What this bride got was a relaxed, intimate affair held in the back garden of her fiancé's house, with local guests invited by phone just a couple weeks ahead. Fortunately, the bride worked in the gourmet food industry, so she was able to get friends in the catering business to provide a beautiful buffet and a gorgeous cake on very short notice. The message? Ask around and see who's got a friend in the business. Connections can help clients as well as businesses. Another bride we know was adamant about keeping her wedding small. She and her fiancé had a low-key but heartfelt civil ceremony. Afterward, the family and friends in attendance shared a meal around a big, round table at a local gourmet

Chinese restaurant. "For us, it was all about making a lifetime commitment—not a bride's big vanity pageant. I wouldn't have had it any other way." San Francisco food columnist Dan Leone and his bride, along with his cousin and his bride's best friend, all piled into his cousin's car and drove down to City Hall to tie the knot. Then, with "That's Amore" coincidentally playing on the car radio, the group headed out to the bride and groom's favorite fried-seafood dive restaurant, "to seal the thing and get grease all over it," celebrating with fried oysters, fried catfish, fried snapper, fried chicken, French fries, hush puppies, gumbo, and peach cobbler. Later, they stopped in at El Rio, the neighborhood bar where they'd first met, and had a wedding toast with a few of their friends. "No frilliness, no fiascos," as Leone put it.

WISHIN' AND HOPIN'

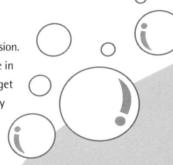

Once you've got a date, start thinking about the occasion. Begin with what you love. You'll have plenty of time in the future to rein in your wedding fantasies. First, get out your notebook and write down every dreamy wedding image you have. Don't be embarrassed if it dates back to your Barbie-and-Ken days. No matter how the image got into your head—a beautiful poem, a sappy movie, an ad in a bridal magazine—write it down, everything from songs to shoes to the color of the rose petals scattered at your feet. Just get it all out there. Take a while to do this. Collect wedding images, and think about what a wedding means to you, without worrying about practicality or price tags. The questionnaire on the facing page will help you tap your inner wedding dreams and desires.

After you've corralled all your visions into a few pages, read through them again. Make a list of the ones closest to your heart. When Stephanie's sister got married, one fantasy image stood fast: she wanted to ride from the ceremony to the reception in a horse-drawn carriage. So the bridal party bounced through the crowded streets of downtown Chicago in three horse-drawn carriages on the Saturday afternoon of her wedding. Sailors waved, city folk gawked—did everyone but the bride feel silly? Sure. But it wasn't their day. What mattered was that the bride felt like a true princess, even when surrounded by lumbering buses and honking taxis. After all, causing traffic jams is a prerogative of royalty, isn't it?

Anti-Bride Fantasy Questionnaire ● ● ● ●

1. I'd like to arrive at my wedding:
   - on horseback
   - walking through a field
   - in a big limo
   - on the back of a motorcycle
   - in a convertible

2. Once I get there, I want to hear:
   - the ocean
   - a string quartet
   - the wind in the trees
   - ethereal trance music
   - Dolly Parton, Merle Haggard, and Emmylou Harris

3. If my wedding were a movie, I'd want it directed by:
   - Nora Ephron
   - Wong Kar-Wei
   - Wim Wenders
   - Jim Jarmusch
   - Pedro Almodovar

4. I would be played by:
   - Audrey Hepburn
   - Lucy Liu
   - Catherine Deneuve
   - Jennifer Lopez
   - Salma Hayek

5. If I could go back in time just for one day you'd find me:
   - in Paris in the 1920s
   - out West with the cowboys
   - in London in the 1960s
   - in Venice during the Renaissance
   - in Shanghai in the 1920s

6. No matter what, at my wedding I want to:
   - feel the breeze in my hair
   - be out in the country
   - be surrounded by lots of sparkling lights and neon (hello, Vegas!)
   - walk down the aisle of a cathedral
   - dance until the sun comes up

Now, ask your spouse-to-be to make his own list. Guys don't usually grow up with anywhere near the amount of wedding baggage that women do, and if he's just popped the question, he probably hasn't thought beyond getting that ring on your finger. But if he's been musing for a while about the prospect of being married to you, he's probably cooked up some images of how he'd like it to happen. Don't try to get your visions to match up yet—just jot down his ideas on a facing page in your notebook. Let them rest there for a while. Then sit down over coffee or a bottle of wine and compare notes. Prioritize your fantasies—see which ones match up, which ones totally clash, and which ones maybe, somehow ("Sure we can rent a horse for the *afternoon*, I know we can!"), might actually work.

WHOSE WEDDING IS IT, ANYWAY?

Unless you run away to Vegas or slink down to City Hall on your lunch break, your wedding won't happen in a vacuum. Once you start letting your friends and family in on your wedding plans, you may be in for a shock. Since they involve so many traditions, weddings can bring out the hidden traditionalist trapped inside even the most progressive people. Don't be surprised if your otherwise reasonably hip siblings, parents, or coworkers suddenly start asking if you've picked out your china pattern, or what song you and your dad are going to dance to at the reception.

Getting the wedding you want—as opposed to the wedding your parents or in-laws think you should have—requires determination, diplomacy, and cash. First off, try to believe that those who are driving you crazy are doing it out of love, not just because they have control issues. Maybe lack of money, wartime, or family opposition prevented your mom from getting the wedding she wanted, and now she's determined to see your wedding done right. Maybe your dad shakes his head at your vintage dress; where you see beautiful tailoring, your father sees someone else's old clothes and feels ashamed for you.

You love your relatives and your friends, and you want them there to celebrate and support your commitment, your responsibility, and your incredibly good luck in finding your soul mate. But just as so many of the traditions of the wedding ceremony focus on the couple's

Wedding Weekend

As you mull over possible dates, think about how important your guests will be in the proceedings. Are you planning a small one-day event that will include only friends and family who live nearby? Or will guests be flying in from far and wide? Are your combined families limited to parents, siblings, and a couple of uncles, or do you have sprawling networks of multiple cousins, aunts, and stepbrothers? More and more, brides and grooms are surrounding their weddings with several days of friend- and family reunions. This takes more planning, since you have to organize not just the wedding but also a vacation for a whole group of people of different ages, interests, and incomes. But the continuation of family traditions (and the creation of new ones) is a central theme for most weddings, so why not celebrate this by taking the time to enjoy your friends and family? Since many families are spread across entire continents these days, just getting to pal around with the ones you love can be a rare treat.

Here's where the Internet can be a godsend: almost every tourist destination or resort area has a Web site stuffed with lodging, dining, and activity suggestions that will make your planning a lot easier. Don't feel that you have to schedule every minute of each day. You're the bride, not Julie the cruise director. Put together a few special activities, but mostly plan on having lots of unstructured time for just kicking back. A barbecue, a softball game in the park, sunset at the beach . . . One of the best wedding memories we have came the night after a friend's wedding, when the whole family convened at the bride's home for an impromptu hootenanny. The bride sang, her aunts played the piano, and the mother of the bride even pulled out her tuba.

Instead of a bachelor or bachelorette party on the night before the wedding, a lot of couples we know are enjoying informal get-togethers that celebrate their community of friends. These can range from a big beachside bonfire to a funny slide show showing the bride and groom during all their most embarrassing moments.

Another great new tradition: yoga classes for the guests! There's nothing like doing a sun salutation or downward-facing dog to work out those pre-wedding kinks. One couple we know offered two classes the morning of their wedding, one at 7:30 and one at 9:30.

creation of a new family unit, the real center of the wedding is you, your spouse, and the person who conducts your ceremony. The three of you are the people who really matter; everyone else's presence is a gift.

Pick Your Battles

If it looks like serious obstacles are going to arise, figure out what three elements are absolutely nonnegotiable for you and your partner. These could be big things: having a civil rather than a religious ceremony; having representatives from both your faiths officiating; or holding the wedding in the city where you live now, rather than in the town where your parents and relatives live. Or they could be little things, such as not wearing a white dress, walking down the aisle alone, or having your best male friend taking the maid-of-honor spot.

Then, figure out what three things are absolutely imperative from your family's point of view. Of course, some of these desires may not be negotiable or even possible to fulfill. Your relatives may wish your fiancé was taller, or Korean, or Catholic—all things that neither they nor you can do anything about. But some of their wishes you may be able to live with, even if you wouldn't have chosen them yourself. These could be as simple as growing out your hair, carrying a bouquet, or, yes, registering for loot at a big-name department store near your grandparents' house, even though you and your beau already have all the wineglasses and salad bowls you need. As any diplomat can tell you, compromise on the little things and you'll have more leverage on the big issues.

> **TIP:** *One bride we know was heavily pressured by her mother-in-law to register at a local department store. So that they wouldn't accumulate tons of unnecessary stuff, she and her fiancé registered for easily returnable items, like towels and cookware, then took the bulk of it back to the store and used the money to extend their honeymoon in Paris for an extra two weeks. Tacky? Perhaps. You be the judge.*

Finally, anyone who's ever had a boss can tell you that the person signing the checks is the one who calls the shots. Weddings can part you from a significant chunk of cash, and financial support from relatives can really help, especially if you're moving into a new apartment or saving for a house. In the long run, though, you'll probably enjoy a less-lavish

Then again, maybe you actually get along with your parents . . .

Of course, getting your family involved in your wedding doesn't have to be all about troubleshooting. Plenty of the brides we spoke with said that getting help from their relatives made the whole day worthwhile.

"My philosophy was to let my mom have as much rein as possible, without going overboard. And it was and always will be MY day, but without her and my father, it wouldn't have been. I saw the event as a communion of lives and not about the glory of two people, but rather everyone together, so the more I asked for help from my family, the more communal and wonderful it became. I was lucky!"

"We got married in an area where there just happened to be no caterers. So we relied on my husband's mother, who designed the entire menu and invited her pals to come do the cooking. Apparently, they had a wonderful time in the kitchen, and the product was amazing."

wedding that really suits your style more than you would a fancier one that feels planned for someone else. And this, conveniently enough, brings us to that unromantic but crucial part of wedding planning, The Budget.

THE STICKER SHOCK

Wedding planning can become distinctly less fun when you realize that every little fairy-tale detail comes with a price tag attached. Even City Hall and a hamburger aren't free; and a designer dress, loads of flowers, and a sit-down dinner for one hundred in a lovely vineyard could easily rival the sum total of your student loans. Unfortunately, if you succumb to the siren call of everything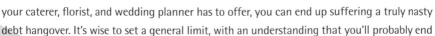
your caterer, florist, and wedding planner has to offer, you can end up suffering a truly nasty debt hangover. It's wise to set a general limit, with an understanding that you'll probably end

up spending about 20 percent more. Figure out beforehand how you're going to pay the bills. Some couples set up a special account for wedding funds to which they both deposit a certain amount each month. If family members wish to contribute, find out (delicately) how much they'd like to give. It's usually less stressful to get the money up front, if possible, rather than having to run the cost of every little thing past those who've offered to contribute. Your aunt may want to pay for your dress, but will she recoil in horror when she realizes that the dress of your dreams is a slinky silver column, not the massive white pouf she had envisioned? Often, money isn't about money; it's about control. By getting the cash in hand, you're cutting whatever strings might have originally been attached. Naturally, this can make some people very uncomfortable, since handing over money can sometimes be a way of making sure they get what they want. So if you think your relatives will put pressure on you and make you uncomfortable, perhaps having the extra cash isn't worth the anguish. We say, do the wedding your way, even if it means giving up that horse and carriage.

HIRING PROFESSIONALS

Sure, you're an ace party thrower. But planning your wedding may be the first time you've engaged professional help. Whether you're booking a caterer, a baker, a florist, a band, or a photographer, you want to get what you want. And the nicest way to do this is to be a good client. This doesn't mean being a pushover; after all, much of what you're paying for is peace of mind. Professional services should deliver what you have asked for, on time and on budget. Unlike wheedling your Uncle Steve to cook up 30 pounds of his famous barbecued ribs, you are *hiring* people to provide what you need, not asking them for a favor.

Be aware, too, that wedding services can cost a lot, and many little details (from renting glassware to hiring valet parkers) can add hundreds of dollars to your overall costs. A good client is one who knows what she wants, knows her budget, and knows where the two will reasonably intersect. Do some shopping around first, and find out the typical price range for the sorts of services you'll need. Caterers, for example, charge by the head, which means that big, super-festive loft party for two hundred could end up eating up a large chunk of change if you insist on filling every table with huge trays of sushi. Don't feel intimidated about stating your budget up front; if a caterer or supplier is truly out of your range, see if they can suggest someone else. If you really want to work with a particular firm, see what options they offer. Could they do a casual buffet instead a sit-down dinner? What about small, seasonal bouquets instead of cascades of white roses? A little flattery never hurts; if you present your wedding as a creative challenge, you may get something much better than you expected. Then again, you may end up with carnations and chips and dip. Go with your gut instincts; don't sign any contracts unless you're absolutely sure you're going to get what you want.

As a recent groom told us, "Don't get suckered into package deals. A lot of times the sales technique is to convince you that you're not in your right mind at the moment, and if you don't go with what they are selling you right then, you will regret it the rest of your life. Don't buy it. There are as many photographers and caterers as there are days before your wedding. Find one who doesn't pressure you." Professionals should be professional; you have every right to expect phone calls to be returned and e-mails and faxes answered. At the same time, remember that you are not this person's only client. It may be your wedding, but to your florist or caterer, it's just one of many jobs. "Bridezilla" is the ugly but apt term used by those in the business for those monster clients who wig out about every little thing. Don't let yourself turn into a bridezilla. No one does his or her best work for a screamer. You're hiring people because they know their jobs; let them do their jobs.

To save all kinds of trouble in the long run, put your agreement in writing. Everything, from the name of the person delivering and setting up the cake to the number of hours you're expecting the band to play, should be specified in the contracts. Keep copies of all of the contracts on file, and assign someone to bring copies to the wedding itself should any last-minute complications arise.

TIP: *Unless you can turn it into a great story, no one at your wedding needs to know what kind of hell you've gone through with the caterers or the florists. What really matters to your guests is that you and your groom show up, take your vows, and smile.*

Warning Signs: Ways to Spot (and Avoid) a
Florist/Caterer/Bandleader from Hell

Be cautious if your florist, caterer, or bandleader matches any of the following descriptions:

- He agrees with everything you say and insists that he can do everything exactly as you want it. Most smart pros know how to gently dissuade clients from impossible (or overly expensive) schemes. Be wary of those who give you a blanket OK, especially if you know that your budget and your brilliant ideas don't exactly match.
- She gets vague when it comes to dollars. Is the catering being charged by the head or by the platter? Does the band get a flat fee or a rate per hour? Those who won't answer these kinds of questions may be planning to explain their suddenly exorbitant fees later by pointing out all the "extras" you agreed upon—items you agreed to without knowing that they were actually in addition to the original calculations.
- He stops returning your phone calls, faxes, or e-mails once the deposit's in.
- She pulls a bait-and-switch. This can happen with florists, and sometimes it's not the florist's fault. The vagaries of nature (and greenhouses) being what they are, certain flowers just aren't available when they're needed. But a good florist will find you something similar in your price range—not make you choose between dyed blue carnations and imported orchids.
- He won't listen to your ideas, claiming, "I am the professional." The worst of these "professionals" will try to convince you that your taste, not theirs, is at fault and that, after all, they have a reputation to uphold. Your wedding is not their portfolio piece.

Ultimately, you're paying: you should get what you want. If any wedding-service provider belittles you, rolls his or her eyes at your ideas, or makes you cry, tear up that check immediately. If you can't get out of a contract, play nice 'til the wedding's over, and then make word of mouth work for you. Call every bride-to-be you know and tell them exactly how you were treated, so they won't make the same mistake.

Friends versus Pros

Many of your pals have probably suffered through scads of dull and/or tasteless events and are just itching to put together a really fabulous party, the way it *should* be done. One of the best ways to make your wedding feel truly personal and memorable is to involve the people you care about. This doesn't mean piling unpaid grunt work onto your pals; instead, think about how they'd like to honor and sweeten your ceremony. By playing a song on the guitar as you walk down the aisle? Singing? Reading poetry? Doing the flowers? If you feel guilty for asking your friends to work, remember this: Participants usually have more fun (and feel much more important) than spectators. Because they know you, they'll have insights into your psyche that no hired decorator or florist could have, whether it's your mystical connection to turtles or your joy in feather boas. That said, cover your butt. If your old roommate promises to do the flowers but suddenly gets dumped by her boyfriend (who just happens to be the groom's best man), she can cry her head off and run to her therapist. Meanwhile, you're sans bouquet, corsage, and centerpiece. Not that you should assume your friends will flake; after all, they love you, and you know where they live. It's just that paying people to do a job helps ensure that they will actually do what they've promised.

Be clear about exactly what you'll need from your pals. If a sweet but wildly irresponsible pal really wants to get involved, find something not terribly important she can do at the last minute, or team her up with a more dependable friend. Regardless, be as organized with friends as you would be with professionals. Be especially clear about who's paying for what, and what your expectations are. If your friend's doing the flowers, make sure she knows your budget and sticks to it. If her artistic vision and your future mortgage payments clash, you might end up combing the flower shops of your neighborhood at six o'clock the night before your wedding trying to find enough daisies and ferns to make two dozen centerpieces. Also, don't let a well-meaning friend get in over her head (see "Deceptively Difficult Items, or What to Leave to the Pros," on page 28). An enthusiastic amateur baker, Stephanie once volunteered to bake a wedding cake for a friend. The cake—a fairly simple three-tiered almond cake—required special pans for baking and extra-large bowls for mixing the gallons of batter. Her oven could hold only one layer at a time, making the baking process a three-hour ordeal. The icing was runny, and, finally, the cake almost didn't fit into the cab. In the end, she missed her friends' ceremony because the whole process took so much more time than she'd anticipated.

Whatever your friends contribute, make sure they also get a chance to just be guests. That way, they can share their talents and have time to drink, flirt, and bask in everyone's congratulations too. Often, the nicest way to do this is to create a ceremony that involves a lot of participation from family and friends. As one bride said, "I'm a writer, so all of our friends read poems that we loved in the wedding ceremony, and the woman who had introduced us sang a song." Having your friends stand up and read quotes from your favorite authors or play your favorite songs can add a truly personal dimension to your event. And even the shyest person can usually manage to channel Julia Roberts or Kenneth Branagh for a minute or two, especially when reading a poem. The rhythm and power of really good poetry speaks for itself: even the most tongue-tied can't mess up the music inherent in the meter.

Whether you're working with friends or pros, work with people you like. You'll have a lot more fun getting that updo from the stylist who's seen you through every impulse, from platinum fuzz to Jennifer Aniston shag, than from some hotshot big name who's only met you once. You need to feel the love.

Do I Need a Wedding Planner?

It depends. Be realistic about how much time you have to devote to making the sort of wedding you want.

Some good reasons for hiring a wedding planner:
• You're planning your wedding in another city or state.
• You have special needs, such as finding a place of worship that will accommodate a mixed-religion ceremony, or tracking down a caterer who can prepare a diabetic-friendly menu.
• You don't have a car, or both you and your fiancé work long hours and travel frequently for business, and you want a big, blowout event.

Relates Stephanie's sister, "My wedding planner did all the research for me. She would pick me up on my lunch hour and drive me to check out three or four different restaurants for the reception, with all of their prices and requirements already written out. All I had to do was make the choices. It was a huge weight off my shoulders." Her wedding planner found a synagogue that would hold a ceremony featuring both a rabbi and a minister, and she also organized that all-important procession of horse-drawn carriages.

PUTTING TOGETHER YOUR BRIDAL PARTY

A bride coming down the aisle preceded by a phalanx of identically attired bridesmaids is still the automatic vision most of us have when we think "wedding." But these days, many brides (and grooms) have mixed-gender groups of attendants. Some brides do away with the whole group altogether, going through their ceremony attended by just one special maid (if she's single) or matron (if she's married) of honor. (If your special pal is a guy, you can call him your honor attendant.) Your sister(s) are traditionally the first ones asked to be in your wedding party, followed by cousins (if you're close) and friends. Similarly, grooms might choose a best friend, a brother, a sister, or a group of pals to stand up with him. It is not necessary for the bride and groom to have exactly the same number of attendants.

Be considerate when you choose your attendants, and be careful to pick people who will find sharing this event with you particularly meaningful. Being a bridesmaid is both an honor and a responsibility, and some women (especially those with a lot of friends around the marrying age) can get burned-out on the whole thing. From the engagement party to the bridal shower to the wedding itself, being in someone else's wedding can eat up a lot of a bridesmaid's time and money. Present the opportunity to your would-be bridesmaids as an invitation, not an ultimatum. In other words, give them a graceful way to decline if they just can't manage it.

Most importantly, think before you pick. Everyone's got that certain friend who just can't help turning every encounter into a one-woman show. You love her—she's totally fun, always lets you borrow her lipstick, and makes any evening into an adventure. But if she goes out for a cup of coffee, she comes home with the phone number of the sexy French guy pulling the lattes; if she walks into a film festival, she'll meet a bunch of guys dying to finance her new video. You know the type. Is she insecure? A pathological liar? Born under a lucky star? Whatever. This is your big day. Don't invite anyone into your bridal circle who'll be spending all her energy trying to out-glam you.

Deceptively Difficult Items, or What to Leave to the Pros

• The cake

Baking and (especially) assembling a wedding cake is much trickier and more time consuming than one might expect, even for accomplished home bakers. All the professional pastry chefs we spoke with told us horror stories about making their first wedding cakes. As a favor to a friend, pastry chef Elizabeth Faulkner created a dramatic, four-tiered cake covered in "stained glass" sugar shards. It was a work of art—until her pal showed up to transport the cake, and Faulkner found herself (and the cake) careening to the wedding in the back seat of a Pinto on a sweltering, 98-percent-humidity June day. If you've got an aunt who's dying to bake something for you, see if she can contribute secondary nibbles, like a big stack of brownies or some beautifully decorated cookies. Or, skip the big cake altogether, and have a potluck "cake table" instead, as described in Chapter 3.

• The photographs

Depending on how much of the ceremony and reception you want documented, your wedding photographer will probably be on the job throughout the entire event. If everyone at the party knows this person as your Uncle Mike or your next-door neighbor, they're going to want to treat him or her as a guest, and you might find it very awkward to have to pull him out of conversations or away from the dinner table. Also, formal portrait-style photography can be technically challenging. If your uncle or your neighbor has his heart set on being the official wedding photographer, consider having wedding portraits taken professionally a few days before or after the wedding. On the actual day, Uncle Mike can snap pictures to his heart's content. Scattering disposable cameras around the reception is the usual way to get these kinds of shots; even more fun are those disposable Polaroid cameras that pop out tiny stickers, which can be added to the wedding album or guest book, or used to dress up your thank-you cards.

Make sure your gals have their priorities straight. Bridal designer Wyndie Nusbaum claims that when she designs for wedding parties, the bridesmaids, not the brides, give her the most trouble. Why? Because with all that love in the air (and friends of the groom on the dance floor), a lot of single women get convinced that they're going to bump into Mr. Right in the conga line. While that might make a great story at *their* wedding, playing matchmaker is not your responsibility. In addition to looking pretty and participating in the actual ceremony, your attendants are there to help out during all the wedding-day events. Along with the groom's best man and attendants, your bridesmaids should be available to guide guests, give special assistance to elderly or disabled guests, and, in general, keep you feeling loved and taken care of throughout the day.

What if you'd love to have your best friend in your wedding party, but right now she's working two jobs in another state to put herself through grad school? There are plenty of graceful ways to get her out to see you without putting an undue strain on her budget. The most direct, of course, is to offer to buy her a ticket. If that's *too* direct (or too bossy), then make the traveling costs her only expense. Find a friend or relative who can put her up for the duration of the wedding events. Tell her that if she'll promise to come to the wedding, she won't have to stand in line at Williams-Sonoma to buy yet another salad spinner. Declare that you're sending her a dress and some dyed-to-match shoes and that if she doesn't show up, they'll haunt the back of her closet forever.

Me and My Shadow

However your wedding party is organized, make sure there's one person who's totally there for you. Whether she's your sister or your best friend, let her know you trust her to anticipate your needs throughout the day. She'll be the one who'll run to get the veil if you leave it in the dressing room, slip you a glass of Champagne when you're wilting in the receiving line, find you a bobby pin, tell you when you've got lipstick on your teeth, and squeeze into the bathroom stall to help you struggle back into your panty hose. In short, she'll be dedicated to keeping a bubble of happy bridal energy around you all day. You won't know beforehand what you'll need, so it's best to pick someone who knows you really, really well. Also, choose someone who's not in high boyfriend-hunting mode. You don't want to be desperately in need of a tissue or a glass of water while your pal is busy chatting up your new brother-in-law.

Me and My MC

Consider appointing someone to be your master or mistress of ceremonies. If you've hired a wedding planner, he or she can often perform this role and double as a troubleshooter during the days leading up to the wedding. On the day of the event, your MC will be the one who deals with the caterers, solves problems, and hands out the checks. The bride and groom should not have to deal with any of these details. Parents are too emotionally involved and are likely to lose their cool. You maid of honor may be too busy taking care of you to notice that someone's toddler just yanked the tablecloth—and all the forks and plates—off the cake stand. You need someone who is alert and ready to prevent disaster (or who knows how to deal with disasters once they happen). Give this person a cell phone, a list of all the vendors participating in the event, and a schedule or timeline of the festivities.

WHO'S THAT GUY?

Let's face it: a lot of the wedding planning is all about you, the bride. It's easy for your guy to feel left out as you grab the phone for the eighteenth call to your sister about the relative virtues of peeled shrimp versus tuna maki for serving at the cocktail reception. Remember, he's getting married too. If he's actually allowed to make some decisions, rather than just being told to drop off a check at the party-rental place, he'll be much less likely to zone out when your to-do deadlines start looming.

GETTING THE LOOT

So, you've been living together since college, and the last thing you need is another toaster. Or, your sweetie's a tiki love god and you're a rockabilly western mama, but your in-laws favor 1980s glitz (track lighting! leather couches!) and your mom adores potpourri. How can you still get fun gifts without ending up with a lot of useless clutter or, worse, six identical salad serving bowls and twenty apple-shaped scented candles? Registering is one way to get a word in before your relatives clobber you with their idea of lovely décor. First, look around your house (or think about the new house or apartment the two of you are planning to share).

Do you really love the towels? Do you like your forks? Do the wineglasses match? Do the napkins? Do you care? A wedding can provide a blameless way for you to upgrade your necessary apartment gear for free. You may feel greedy or uncomfortable roaming the aisles of Williams-Sonoma or Target with that price-code zapper gun. However, you're actually making it easier on out-of-town guests, especially if they're family members who don't really see you in your day-to-day life. And if your friends or family have been dying to see you replace those burlap-shaded Goodwill lamps, a registry can help prevent everyone from buying you the same stack of Ikea stuff. But don't feel limited to housewares. Lots of couples set up registries for sports equipment, traveling gear, hobby-related items, home electronics, you name it. If a new Sony PlayStation will go far in ensuring marital harmony, ask for it. A lot of on-line stores, like Amazon, now offer the opportunity to make a "wish list" of books, CDs, and dozens of other items.

Some guests may whine that they're terrible at choosing wedding presents. Well, remember how your mom always insisted that she liked handmade gifts best (even if this meant receiving unidentifiable objects made of Styrofoam, macaroni, and glitter)? She really did appreciate the time and care you put into making those gifts. And when it comes to your wedding, some friends will want to do something a little more personal for you. Let your friends know how cool it would be if they made you something instead of just going on-line with a credit card (no pressure of course). Consider encouraging enterprising friends by giving them a special task. For example, Carolyn makes a mean glögg, a warming Scandinavian drink of spiced wine and spirits. For one couple, instead of giving the usual martini shaker or waffle iron, Carolyn whipped up a big batch of glögg. Empty Grolsch beer bottles (the kind with self-closing caps) made perfect containers, especially when adorned with the special labels she designed herself.

As we said earlier, be wary of dumping all the grunt work of your wedding on your family and friends. That advice still holds. If they are genuinely interested in doing something special for your wedding, make it clear that you view their help as a wedding present. Whether they're driving a U-Haul full of rented folding chairs or setting up the sound equipment, friends who really come through for you when you need it are giving you the absolute best present anyone

Or why not ask for . . .

- *Opera, symphony, or ballet tickets (a group of friends can chip in for a season-long subscription)*
- *A gift certificate good for a weekend at a favorite inn, cabin, or bed-and-breakfast*
- *A case of a favorite wine, or membership in a special wine club*
- *That dreamy velvet chaise lounge or way-cool painting from your favorite store or gallery (just in case your family decides they want to chip in and buy you something big)*
- *Items you love to collect, whether they're vintage Barbie dolls or 1930s fruit-print tablecloths (good kitsch being widely available via the Internet)*
- *Favorite cuttings, seeds, or plants for your garden*
- *Glamorous yet unnecessary items: a vintage martini shaker, brandy snifters, a punch bowl with matching cups, a big beautiful mirror, or copper pots*
- *Fun stuff for the honeymoon: a rental-car upgrade to a Porsche or vintage Jag, a night in a really lavish hotel, dinner for two in a great restaurant, or a sailboat cruise or scuba expedition*
- *Swing- or salsa-dancing lessons*
- *Cooking classes at a local culinary school or gourmet shop (even if you know the basics, why not expand your repertoire to include unfamiliar realms—Thai food, for example, or fabulous homemade pastry?)*

can give to a bride and groom: peace of mind. Let them know this ahead of time and thank them accordingly.

Another fun option is an arts-and-services "registry." Ask your artist friends to give you something from their own studio—a story, a film, a painting, a photograph, a piece of sculpture, furniture, pottery, or a song (not the band's demo tape but a song they've written for the occasion). Sound interesting? You'll actually be reviving the elegant tradition of the epithalamium, a song or poem composed in honor of a wedding. John Donne wrote these, as did Keats and Shelley. If a friend has a fabulous skill, like creating astrological charts or giving massages, ask for a chart reading or a pre-wedding rubdown. One bride we know had a friend who was a pagan priestess do a cleansing and welcoming ritual at the couple's new house. Another had a photographer friend shoot a portrait of her, her husband, and their brand-new baby. This way, your friends share what they have to spare—talent and time—while hanging onto the cash they need to pay the rent and buy their paints.

Tacky Behavior and How to Avoid It

No matter how much you may be looking forward to throwing out all those mismatched washcloths and thrift-store wineglasses, etiquette requires that you act gracious and surprised when you become the lucky recipient of a set of monogrammed leopard-print placemats. In addition, you shouldn't list the stores where you've registered on the wedding invitations. While it may seem like a practical way to let people know where to go to buy presents, it sends the message that guests are expected to cough up a gift. Even though it may be equally bad form for a wedding guest *not* to send a gift, listing the registry up front makes the whole project look a little too commercial. Let a few high-profile people know where you're registered—your mom, your maid of honor, the best man—and let them spread the news to those who ask.

Asking for cash—contributions to a down-payment fund for a home purchase or toward your honeymoon trip—is a delicate matter. If you were previously married or have been living together for a long time, you may already have all the flatware and lamps you need. Even so, it's not your guests' responsibility to pay your mortgage or send you to Belize. Some guests, especially if they're older relatives, will indeed feel it's only right to cushion the shocks of your new married life with a nice fat check. But it's much more graceful not to ask. Don't let all the attention lavished on you, the bride-to-be, inflate your sense of entitlement. We'd all like to get big chunks of cash just for being who we are; that's why so many people try to get their memoirs published. Don't equate "presence" with "presents." No matter how fabulous a party you throw, your guests only owe you the former, not the latter.

Giving Thanks

Writing thank-you notes is a little like removing your mascara before you go to sleep. It's just the right thing to do. It only takes a couple of minutes, but it seems like a huge pain until you actually get it over with. It's only when you wake up with those raccoon eyes—or feel that nagging sense of guilt when you use your brand-new waffle iron—that you realize procrastination is a road paved with regret, remorse, and unused stamps. Make the job easier by ordering a big box of thank-you notes when you order your wedding invitations. When the presents start to arrive, keep a log of who sent what gift. Mark down the guest's name, address, and the item they sent. Then, after the wedding, spend some after-dinner time each night tackling five or ten names on the list. The basic formula? A general thank-you for the gift, a specific mention of what you liked about it or how you plan to use it, and a brief line about how much you enjoyed seeing them at the wedding or (if they didn't attend) how you hope they're doing well. If they sent cash, mentioning their "generous gift" is more graceful than saying, "Thanks for showing us the money!" If you can, pass on a cheery hint as to what you are planning to do with the dough. Going to Paris? Buying a new bass for the band? Repairing the porch? Let the givers know.

HONEYMOON

In the midst of all your wedding planning, take a few days off to plan the most important part: the honeymoon! Finally, no relatives, no stress—just the two of you with nothing to do all day but enjoy each other's company. Whether you reserve on-line or go through a travel agent, be sure to make your plans with plenty of time to get good fares and rates. Although it's traditional for the bride and groom to leave in a flurry of rice and good wishes, you don't have to start your honeymoon immediately after the wedding. Some couples we know followed their wedding with a weekend in a great hotel, setting off to Paris or Costa Rica a few weeks or months after the wedding. Annie and Craig, who run a small but very popular restaurant in San Francisco, couldn't afford to leave their business running on its own for several weeks. Instead, they planned "honeymoon days" during the months after their wedding, escaping from the city for a couple of days every few weeks. Another couple, Amy and Tom, advised, "Tell everyone, from the woman at the car rental agency to the flight attendants on the plane, that you and your new husband are on your honeymoon. We did, and people went out of their way to help us out and make our trip special." From a bottle of Champagne in your hotel room to a first-class upgrade on the plane, all the honeymooners we talked to had received VIP treatment just for being newlyweds. (Also, when you're planning, don't forget all the little stuff to take care of at home, like finding a pet-sitter and stopping your mail.)

Where to go? Think about what you both like to do best. Hike? Surf? Stroll through the city? Even if you've always dreamed of going to Prague or backpacking through Nepal, keep in mind that your honeymoon should be as stress free as possible. Weddings are exhausting, and you may not want to be running around beforehand getting malaria shots or applying for your visa. You don't want your special time together usurped by the demands of travel in a difficult place. We recommend planning something less complicated or demanding. Instead of scuba lessons in the morning and reef diving in the afternoon, leave plenty of time to just do nothing. Not only will you need it, you'll enjoy it. And we'd be willing to guess that once you catch up on your sleep you'll come up with a few fun ways to pass the time. Just don't forget to hang out that "do not disturb" sign!

ONE FINAL NOTE

Remember to go on dates. And no, going to the department store to look at flatware patterns isn't a date. Don't let the wedding preparations take over your lives, especially if you and your fiancé are already living together. Granted, unless you regularly entertain heads of state, putting your wedding together probably involves more planning, negotiations, long-distance phone calls, and appointments than any other event you've ever put on. But, at the same time, remember that governments will not topple if you can't find the exact cake topper you wanted. Is anyone really going to remember whether the wedding cake had raspberry or mocha buttercream filling? Make sure all the romantic, fun stuff you two like to share together—whether a Sunday-morning run around the lake or a Monday-night pool game—doesn't disappear under a pile of wedding magazines.

Places and Spaces: From Barns to Boats

A flower-filled meadow, salty breezes, glowing tents glittering with sparkly lights . . . now's your chance to make those dreams come true. It helps to have your weekends free during this part of the planning, because you'll probably be covering a lot of miles as you begin comparing your fantasy with the realities of head counts and parking access.

What comes first, the guest list or the location? Obviously, where you can have your wedding will depend on the number of guests you plan to invite. We think that being surrounded by your tribe will probably be the most important and memorable aspect of your wedding, so we suggest you make your guest list first, then start searching for a place where you can squeeze them all in. You may revise that list down the road, depending on what you can find (and afford), but put the people first.

ALWAYS ROOM FOR ONE MORE . . .

Before you start looking for a space for your ceremony and reception, write down the name of every single person you're thinking of inviting, including their spouses and partners. Wouldn't it be lovely if they could all be there? But the cruel truth is that the cost of everything at a wedding event, from renting the space to serving the cake, is figured out on a per-head basis. You know those swell folks who've birthed, raised, and befriended you through all these years? To a caterer, they're all just heads. Depending on where you'd like to get married, and how much you can afford to spend, some heads may have to roll in order for the production to happen. Although you won't know the exact number of guests you'll be hosting until the RSVPs come in, you should be able to get a ballpark figure from your rough list. You *did* remember to ask your fiancé to pitch in with his list, too, right?

So now you've got your initial, all-inclusive list, give or take a few names. Sharpen that pencil or get a couple of different font colors going on your laptop. Imagine you're the door girl at Asia de Cuba at ten o'clock on a Friday night. You get to decide who gets in and who's going to end up watching late-night television again. Put two stars next to the names of the true

VIP guests—your parents, your sister, your fiancé's brother and sister-in-law, your best friend, etc., and so forth. Put one star next to the names of those people whom you'd really like to include but are not absolutely duty-bound to invite. These make up your "A" and "B" lists. The unstarred guests go into a third category, the wish list. If money and space get tight, the wish list will be aptly named, because you'll be saying, "I *wish* we could invite cousin Linda and her six Jack Russell terriers, but we'd have to cash in all our stock options and serve mashed potatoes from KFC in order to feed everyone."

However you create your lists, you and your fiancé will need to agree on the criteria for deciding who's included and who's not. For some couples, this means including only those people who are friends of both parties. So yes on your mutual Sunday-night poker group, but no to his frat buddies and your book-group pals. Others split it right down the middle— thirty guests for you, thirty guests for me. One couple limited their wedding to those who were involved in their life on a regular basis. Far-flung friends didn't make it; those they saw every week, or every few weeks, did.

FINDING THE RIGHT PLACE

Now you can start your location search with a few figures in mind. Your "A" list might contain thirty people, your "A" and "B" lists together might contain sixty, and your "A," "B," and wish

The Ex Question

Unless you two have been sweethearts since second grade, each of you is bound to have some significant others in your past. Which of these ex-boy- and ex-girlfriends get to come? This is something you two have to hammer out, and the sooner the better. Be honest: If there's one ex-girlfriend in your beau's life who drives you insane, admit it. But it may be unreasonable to ask that all exes be banished. Emphasizing that all your exes are now happily married, rapidly balding, or gay can help. Be reasonable and ready to compromise.

lists together might total eighty-five people. You'll be able to rattle these numbers off when you make your first round of calls.

Before you pick up the phone, start thinking about the ceremony. You probably already know whether you'll be having a religious ceremony. If you want to have a religious ceremony but you don't already belong to a particular house of worship, keep in mind that many places require couples to attend its services, receive instruction, and become part of its community of faith before they can be wed there. Others may be more open, but almost every place gives scheduling priority to members of their own community. Before you get your heart set on that sweet, little country church or historic synagogue, talk to the minister, pastor, or rabbi in charge and find out what they require.

Most places of worship have an area available for receptions and special events. However, these are often utilitarian spaces, built to resist the destructive forces of decades of second graders just released from Sunday school. If you decide to hold your reception elsewhere, get a map and draw a circle around the ceremony location to help you determine how close or far away your reception should take place. You don't want people to have to drive more than twenty or thirty minutes to get to the second part of the event.

If you're going to have a nondenominational or civil ceremony, you'll have a truly mind-blowing array of choices. Try to narrow down your vision somewhat—indoors or out, summer or winter, an afternoon tea or a big dance-party blowout. Calling up a few of your dream locales and finding out what they charge for hosting one hundred people on a June weekend should help narrow your choices down even further, unless money (and your lead time) is no object. Places with everything available—a charming locale, beautiful gardens, big prep kitchens, wheelchair-accessible bathrooms—will charge for it. That's why they're in the rental business.

If you're feeling a little tentative about the whole process, make some appointments to see some standard wedding-rental sites in your area. Flip through a comprehensive event-site guidebook like *Here Comes the Guide*, which covers regions in California, or look for local ads in the back of bridal magazines. Once you get a sense of what these places offer and how much their services cost, you'll have a better idea as to what you do and don't want in a wedding environment. You can also get a sense of how you and your fiancé want to be treated.

Are the staffs at these sites treating you like potential clients? Or like little lambs being readied for the (very lucrative) slaughter? After your fifth trip around the waterfall/grape arbor/koi pond, you and your fiancé may also realize that, no matter what luxuries are offered, these places are absolutely wrong for your wedding. At this point, you've got two choices: start looking in less-typical places, or have your event at home.

Offbeat Spaces

If you can rent it, you can probably have your wedding there. While hotels, inns, and resorts are the most typical places to hold weddings, every town has dozens of less obvious (and often much less expensive) locations that be turned into fabulous party spaces. Here are a few of our favorites:

- Small, family-run vineyards
- Grange halls
- Film studios
- Art museums
- Galleries
- Ski lodges in the off-season
- Veterans' halls and Legion halls
- Private restaurant dining rooms
- Historic boats moored in a marina (this way, no one's trapped or seasick)
- Municipal parks or civic auditoriums
- Historic homes
- Theaters
- University chapels
- Band shells
- Libraries
- Clubs and meeting halls
- Your favorite funky bars or clubs
- Barns adjoining small farms or orchards
- Corporate rooftop gardens or terraces

Think about the weddings you've attended or heard about in your area. Which ones were super-cool, and why? What worked about the space, and what didn't? Now start making the rounds. Start with your city Chamber of Commerce or Visitors' Bureau. Sometimes, as a resident, you might not even know about some of your hometown's best attractions. All kinds of places are up for grabs for an afternoon.

If you're planning an outdoor wedding, take a walk through the parks, scenic spots, and hiking areas around where you live. One memorable wedding we attended was held in a wooded recreation area. Guests walked up a short trail to find a group of chairs set up in a shady grove.

The ceremony took place under the trees. Afterward, guests walked back down to find a dozen decorated picnic tables and a cold buffet luncheon set out. Then, using a portable generator, a DJ played some fun dance music, turning a flat dirt space into a rocking dance floor.

Loved strolling through that organic apple orchard you discovered during a recent road trip? Give the owners a call. Farming being what it is, a lot of small farms, orchards, and vineyards now depend on "agri-tourism" to keep them in business, whether that means offering seasonal cooking classes, selling apple pies and doughnuts, or hosting weddings. Resorts known for one thing, such as skiing, can be very reasonably priced and accommodating in the off-season. Places that do most of their business in the evenings, like bars and clubs, can also be much more affordable during the afternoon.

Making It Yours

What if you find a place you love, but you aren't sure if it's really the right place for you? Choosing a space is a little like apartment hunting—even when it's love at first sight, it's hard to sign the papers if you haven't shopped around for a while. Of course, shopping around takes time, and while you're looking, other couples are booking. If you find a space you like, ask whether you can put down a refundable deposit to hold the date. Make sure that the person in charge writes down—in ink—the date until which they'll hold the booking. Note the amount of the deposit, so that you can be sure that it is applied toward your final payment should you decide to go ahead with the booking. As always, get *everything* in writing.

Once you decide on a space, be certain you're clear on the number of hours you'll have it, from setup to cleanup. Just because you've put down a deposit, don't assume that your location is yours for the entire day. If you've booked the space for the afternoon, find out if there's another event scheduled for the evening. Make sure you know when you're expected to be out, and what time the setup people for the next event will be arriving. Also, know the cancellation terms, and make sure to mark any deadlines down in your planner so you can get your money back should any of your wedding plans go awry before the big day.

Some places have arrangements with specific caterers, serving staffs, and food and beverage companies. If you're planning on doing a potluck, or bringing in your favorite wine from a friend's vineyard, clear it with the location managers first. Likewise, if you're having live music, find out whether the location has sufficient electricity, setup space, and the proper city permits (e.g., for amplified sound or live entertainment) for the type of band you'll be bringing.

TIP: *Think about the flexibility of the reception you're imagining. How much socializing will you be doing? You'll be able to circulate a lot more at a buffet brunch or cocktails-and-dancing party than at a formal sit-down dinner.*

HOME, SWEET HOME

Having a wedding at home (yours or your parents) can save you a lot of stress. Obviously, you'll know where everything is, and you won't have to pay a rental fee. But it's also very important to go through your home with the same checklist you'd use for a rental space. The first issue you'll need to address is whether the home has enough available space to hold the ceremony and the party. If it does, then see what answers you come up with for the following lists:

Parking
- Where will the guests park their cars?
- Will they be able to park without blocking the neighbors' driveways or parking spaces?
- Will guests' cars be safe in the neighborhood?

Access
- Are the stairs, driveways, steps to the backyard, and other passages safe and well lit?
- Is there enough indoor and outdoor lighting, especially along the driveway and paths leading to the house?
- Is there full access for elderly or disabled guests? Can a ramp be fitted over the front steps, if needed?

Space and Electricity

- Are there enough outlets for microphones, extra lighting, and band equipment?
- Is there enough storage and prep room in the kitchen?
- Do the freezer and fridge have room for all the food and beverages?

Meet and Greet

- Is there a place where guests can be greeted?
- Where will the coats go?
- Is there a place for a gift table?
- Is there a place for moms to nurse and/or change babies, or for small children or elderly folks to rest?

Bathrooms

- Are there enough bathrooms?
- Is there a bathroom on the ground floor, and is it safe and accessible to disabled or elderly guests?
- If a guest has a nurse or caregiver, can that person fit comfortably into the bathroom to provide help if needed?
- Is the plumbing or septic system up to heavy usage? (This is a particularly important issue to resolve in old or out-in-the-country houses.)

Depending on how you feel about your childhood, you may love the idea of going back to your parents' house to tie the knot. Or you might want to take the advice of an event planner we know, who believes that returning to the same backyard where your brother buried your Barbies is *not* the best way to show off your now-chic and grown-up self. Keep in mind that "home" doesn't have to mean *your* home. Ask around to find out who among your family or friends might have a house and/or yard to put at your disposal. Think about the people you know who've been blessed with a summer house, a chunk of lakefront property, or a spacious spread up in the mountains. If appropriate, let slip how hard a time you're having finding the perfect wedding location, and keep your fingers crossed that they'll take the bait. If they do, proceed with caution and with utmost respect. Tying the knot at Aunt Marie's seaside estate isn't worth ruining the good relationship you have with her and Uncle Larry. Whatever you choose, make sure that the site has plenty of room for everyone. We think the sexiest space is a backyard that's big enough to get lost in. Finally, no matter how much you get seduced by a heart-stopping view or sweeping vista, remember to keep these two questions in mind when you think about your ceremony: Will people feel comfortable where they're sitting (or standing)? And will they be able to see the people they're honoring—namely, you and your new spouse? If not, keep looking.

TIP: *Get friendly with a local car club, and have all your wedding attendants driven to the event in vintage muscle cars or swanky 1950s big-finned road boats.*

ETIQUETTE STUFF

Cell Phones and Cameras

We'd like to hope that no guest would actually use a cell phone during a wedding ceremony except to call for help if the bride's veil caught on fire. However, some people are just a little too fond of these new toys, and so putting a note in the program asking guests to turn off all devices of this nature is perfectly OK.

Use of cameras can also be handled this way. As glamorous as it might seem to others, the constant clicking of camera shutters and angling video-camera operators can be very distracting. You don't want to feel stalked by paparazzi at your own wedding. Decide what your attitude is beforehand, and ask your ushers (or designate a few friends) to enforce it. A note in the program followed by a discrete whisper in the ear of the most obvious snappers can go far toward preserving your sanity. After all, you want to be thinking lofty thoughts about undying love and devotion, which is close to impossible if you're worrying about whether your forehead's gotten shiny already.

Screamers and Squealers

A lot of ink in "Miss Manners" and "Dear Abby" is devoted to letters written by brides looking for polite ways to keep the under-ten set away from their expensive weddings. Unfortunately, there really is no polite way to specify this (other than omitting the children's names on the invitation envelopes). Babies are actually the least of your worries. Since they're not mobile yet, they stay where you put them (usually in a sling, a baby carrier, or a portable car-seat), and a good dose of milk or formula (what one new mom calls "nursing into oblivion") usually puts them into a ceremony-long snooze. Oddly enough, a baby's wails at a wedding are seen by some as charming. The same people who, on a crowded airplane, would hiss and shoot evil looks at the parents tend to laugh indulgently here (probably because they're assuming that it's only a matter of time before you swap that fancy gown for an old T-shirt with baby spit-up running down the back). Officiants who are old hands at this sort of thing—like ministers or rabbis—can be counted on to trot out a few stock jokes to smooth over any squealing interruptions. However, if the baby really starts screaming, your ushers should gracefully assist the mom or dad in question to a place away from the ceremony where they can calm Junior down without holding up the event.

Toddlers are a different story. Mobile, full of energy, and having attention spans the length of a TV commercial, two- to four-year-olds shouldn't be expected to sit through something as tedious and grown-up as a wedding ceremony. The most graceful way to get this across to the parents is not to focus on yourself ("I *do not* want the reception hall trashed by your undisciplined brats") but on the little darlings themselves ("Oh, don't you think this will be *hugely boring* for Tyler and Emma? It's going to be such a *long* ceremony, and I don't think any other kids will be there for them to play with. My cousin knows a great baby-sitter who could take care of them for the afternoon—want me to give her a call?").

In the same category as destructive kids (but, alas, much less cowed by the threat of a time-out in the car and no wedding cake) are badly behaved guests—the ones who drink too much, air family grievances at inappropriate moments, or commandeer the mike during the toasts. What do you do when a guest really gets really out of hand? Make this bad guest someone else's responsibility; as the bride, you already have enough to do without being the mom of the party. Even better, you could try to prevent the problem from arising in the first place.

If you know that one or more of your guests might be a handful, be sure to alert someone beforehand. This is a good job for your groom's best man—he doesn't have to be a bouncer, just able to run a little damage control before things get really crazy. Few people come to weddings alone; the best man might try to find the person closest to the monster guest and see if that unlucky person can get them back under control.

Drinking and Driving: No, No, No

Do not, under any circumstances, let guests drive home drunk. If your reception is taking place in an out-of-the-way location far from your guests' homes or hotels, please include some form of transportation—taxis, cars and drivers, or a rented van or bus—in your wedding planning.

REAL WEDDINGS

How did they do it? The coolest ideas we found came from couples who planned their weddings their way—and lived to tell about it. Here, you can take a quick trip through some very different but thoroughly awesome weddings and find out how they happened.

A Wiccan Handfasting

As a founding editor of *Wired* magazine, Kristin knew all about how to be a hip twenty-first-century gal. But for her wedding, she wanted to get in touch with the spiritual side she'd developed through her involvement in a Wiccan circle. She and her husband, Colin, pledged their troth in a traditional Wiccan handfasting. In this ritual, the couple chooses how long they wish to be together. In the highest option, a lifetime handfast symbolically binds the souls of the couple together for lifetimes to come; this was the option Kristin and Colin chose.

Two days before the wedding, the couple held a private "cord ceremony." The members of their ritual circle each brought along a ribbon, leather strip, or chain six feet long. For this event, each of the seven elements was called upon: the four directions, plus above, below, and center. Each person went around the circle and spoke a blessing on his or her cord as a "gift" to the bride and groom. Each person then gave Kristin and Colin his or her cord, symbolizing that the couple could always call on the communal wisdom of their family and friends.

On the day of their wedding, the couple entered a redwood grove to the sound of uilleann pipes (Irish bagpipes), with the groom wearing a kilt and the bride wearing a long, green velvet dress. A Wiccan priestess bound together the couple's hands with the braided cords from the cord ceremony. (The modern term "tying the knot" comes from this handfasting ritual.) Then, Kristin and Colin jumped over a broom (another Wiccan tradition, also adopted by African American slaves, who were forbidden to legally marry). Their broom was decorated with roses, ivy, and lavender. Following the ritual, the broom was passed around to all the guests, each of whom wished for great things for the couple—like always finding a perfect parking space!

Culture Club in a State Park

Gino and Carola were married in April. Having just opened a restaurant, they were short on cash, but given their close-knit families, they knew they couldn't get married without a big party. So, they reserved a section of a nearby state park. Friends chipped in to create a giant potluck buffet and bar that reflected Gino's Lebanese background and Carola's Mexican heritage. Shish kebabs were washed down with tequila, and *mojitos* (a refreshing rum drink spiked with mint) clinked next to bowls of hummus. Because Carola is a professional flamenco dancer and teacher, she and her students performed a lively flamenco dance, and everyone joined in. After that, a belly dancer did a scarf dance, which also included plenty of audience participation.

Old-World Romance

Carolyn's friends Mike and Ellen got married in a garden near the old Annapolis Naval Cemetery. Before the wedding, Carolyn art-directed an impromptu photo shoot of the bride and groom traipsing among the headstones, throwing flowers, and kissing chastely. The sea air, the romantic ambiance, and the reunion of old college friends made it a magical September afternoon. There was no dancing; the guests just sat under a canopy of golden autumn leaves, drinking twelve-year-old Scotch and reconnecting with old and dear friends.

A Mountaintop Idyll

Chris, a DJ and musician, and Allison, a teacher and artist, had a wedding rooted in ancient traditions but with a contemporary vibe, supported by a whole community of friends and family. For the site they chose the Wildwood Retreat, a rustic mountaintop lodge near Guerneville, California. They rented the entire lodge for their event, so it became their own under-the-redwoods paradise, with hot tubs, camping areas, and a great swimming pool. They kept the number of people in attendance to sixty, inviting family and those friends they had in common.

The ceremony took place in a beautiful spot with 270-degree views of the surrounding mountains and river valley. The centerpiece of the wedding was a custom-made metal altar that Allison had commissioned from a sculptor in her neighborhood. Made of recycled metal and glass beads, it featured a spiral design and a theme of fire and water to represent the bride's and groom's astrological signs. (They planned to turn it into a gazebo in their garden after the wedding.) Guests were seated in a spiral, with the altar in the center. The ritual began with the wedding party following the spiral path to the altar, the men carrying cedar branches and the women carrying flowers. Music played by friends on sitar, flute, banjo, and mandolin accompanied the procession. Chris entered with his mom; Allison came in with both her parents and her dog.

Chris and Allison had written their vows together, early on the morning of the wedding. Allison spoke of the rings in a tree as a metaphor for the cycle of life, and the eternity of love. Chris spoke of the grooves on a record, and the eventual "lock groove" of love (the spot at the end of a record where the needle goes around and around endlessly, just like his love for her). Then, their friends "wove" a poem around them, each one speaking a line of poetry while circling around the couple three times. After the vows, family members read poems and another friend performed a flute solo. Finally, Chris stomped on a glass (as in the Jewish tradition) and a circle of friends asked the guests, "Do you take Chris and Allison?"

Über Tradition

Niall and Jean, former mods and punkers from Washington, D.C., decided to rebel in a different way: by having a super-traditional wedding. Niall, a fine Scottish boy, ordered a kilt made of his family's tartan. The bride wore her grandmother's wedding dress. They married in a converted barn in Vermont, the home state of the bride. Because Niall is the Midwest regional director for an Italian vineyard, they served sensational wines. Of course, bagpipes were played for the processional.

Lounge Lizards

Carolyn and Laurent are urban cats who'd rather be in a deep leather banquette sipping a cocktail than, well, practically anywhere. For their celebration location they chose a swanky bar in San Francisco's North Beach. They hired two DJs: one who spun Tito Puente, Latin soul, and bossa nova; and one who brought along some P-Funk, Troublefunk, and 1970s soul. Friends pitched in on every aspect of this event: one arranged the flowers and drove Carolyn around to do wedding errands on his motorcycle; another helped design the menu and cooked for two days before the wedding.

University Union

The day before her wedding, Amy and all her bridesmaids steamed, splashed, and relaxed at a hot tub–spa in Palo Alto, California. The next day, the ceremony was held around the water temple on the campus of Stanford University. The bride and groom walked along the lovely long pool to the ceremony site, a classical "temple" surrounded by Italian marble columns. The guests were seated on either side. After the wedding, the group walked from the university into town for a luncheon reception in the garden of a nearby women's club.

San Francisco Style

Abby and Jack wanted to have an urban wedding that celebrated the feeling of San Francisco, their chosen hometown. Their ceremony was held at the Presidio's nondenominational chapel tucked in a eucalyptus grove in this former Army base, now a national park. After the ceremony, guests piled into a motorized cable car and rode to a cocktail reception in the café at the Palace of the Legion of Honor (one of San Francisco's most beautiful art museums). Although the museum was closed, guests were able to view the paintings and sculptures surrounding the café.

Ambiance: Style Central

Designing your wedding—from the invitations and the decorations to the meal and the all-important cake—can be a fun, creative, and, yes, exhausting endeavor. So many choices! Cream laid paper or shadow-printed vellum? Rose petals or Mylar confetti? Plastic forks and spoons or silver settings? Surf band or swing? We talked to dozens of brides, stylists, bakers, and bands to get their coolest ideas for you. So mix, match, and, of course, get it in writing.

THEMES AND VARIATIONS

Strawberries, white tablecloths, smoked salmon, Champagne, wedding cake, a harpist, and a cello player . . . these can make a lovely wedding reception. But you could also set up a fabulously draped tent, scatter huge, gorgeous pillows everywhere, set out brass platters of hummus and pita bread, and turn your event into a Moroccan fantasy. Theme weddings can be tons of fun, and they're often a lot less stultifying than those that take the usual excruciatingly tasteful route. Of course, you'll want to pick a theme that connects with the way you live, but here are a few ideas to get you thinking.

Rockabilly Western Wedding

Stephanie's friends Jill and Owen front a country-and-western band called Red Meat. So it was only fitting that their wedding took place in a small-town country bar and barbecue restaurant—the sort of place that has a plaque on the wall commemorating the huge buffalo barbecue of a few years back. A big grill was set up in the parking lot, everyone danced, and at least half a dozen bands turned the whole event into an old-fashioned hootenanny.

> **TIP:** *Set up a big horseshoe lit with lots of Vegas-style lights where couples can have their picture taken.*

South Seas Paradise

Transform any backyard into a Polynesian paradise. Hand out leis at the door, rent lots of potted palms, and light the yard with lots of flaming tiki torches. Set up portable palm-frond huts around the bar and the buffet, and make sure to have lots of tiny cocktail umbrellas and cherry-and-pineapple garnishes on hand for drinks. Hire a surf band or get a DJ to spin lots of classic exotica music and Hawaiian slack-key guitar tunes.

Arabian Nights

Piles of silky cushions take the place of chairs here, or you can cover couches and banquettes with Oriental rugs and long swaths of brocade. Serve finger foods like olives, stuffed grape leaves, hummus with warm pita-bread triangles, and baklava on round brass-colored trays. Then bring out delectable platters of lamb and swordfish kebabs and couscous. Finish with wedges of melon and grapes drizzled with rose water. Spicy incense and North African and Middle Eastern music complete the festivities.

Garden Party

Think *Brideshead Revisited*; think *The Great Gatsby*. Ask your guests to put on their best summer pastels; straw boaters and parasols optional. A Dixieland ragtime band or jazz combo can keep things hopping while guests circulate with glasses of Champagne and iced tea. Loads of roses spill out across white linen tables. Guests nibble on tea sandwiches, strawberries and cream, and petit fours. If the party stretches on into the evening, strings of multicolored Japanese lanterns can illuminate the celebration.

Cocktail Groove

Kiss, kiss, darling! Sparkle plenty at this glamour do. No sitting down here—keep guests on their feet so they can get maximum schmoozing time. Suggest elegant cocktail attire on your swanky invitations. Have a few waiters on hand to keep those yummy snacks coming—from tasty grilled shrimp to mini-burgers. And make sure everyone's got a brimming glass of the night's signature cocktail—the better to toast you with, of course! Some good grooves in the background will keep the party going well into the wee hours of the morning.

Into the Woods

Have a *dejeuner sur l'herbe* in a sunlit forest grove. Set up tables under the trees and drape them with sheer white linens. Let ivy and flowering vines trail over the tables, and serve foods connected to the earth: wild-mushroom tart, grilled quails, a salad sprinkled with edible flowers, a rich walnut cake. A small quartet can provide ambient music, or just let the wind blowing through the trees supply the background sound.

Where the Wild Things Are

Create an altar with willow branches woven with berry-laden boughs, and decorate it with moss, acorns, and leaves. Cluster small tables on the grass, each draped in a different shade of fabric and decorated with birdcages filled with toy animals. Encourage guests to come in casual dress, and slip off their shoes when they arrive. Mandolin and dulcimer music will maintain that fanciful mood.

INVITATIONS

Sure, you can do the usual cream-and-black engraved thing. But with so many great materials out there, anyone with a speck of artistic talent can play around with a good design program, a scanner, and a color printer and come up with a fun and personal invite. If you are planning a theme for your wedding, design your invitation to reflect that theme. Take a spin through a well-stocked art-supply store, and you'll find dozens of papers, inks, materials (like shiny Mylar or glittery acetate), and festive add-ins (like tiny stars and sparkly confetti). You don't have to limit yourself to something that fits into an envelope. One bride we know mailed her invitations in aluminum tins, with sheer ribbons wrapped around the paper invitations inside.

Along with paper invitations, more and more couples are choosing to create wedding Web sites that list all the wedding information and include easy links to on-line maps and travel-planning services. (If you're registered on-line, it's up to you whether or not to add links to those stores. Some etiquette experts think this is tacky. Others think you're saving your guests time and trouble. It's really up to you.)

However, it's still pretty much *de rigueur* to send out official invitations by snail mail. Computers crash, URLs get lost, and, however useful it may be for keeping in touch with your brother in Bangkok, e-mail is still too casual and too ephemeral for wedding invitations. If you're really pressed for time and your wedding is going to be an intimate affair, get on the phone. A personal telephone invitation is preferable to an electronic one.

Printed invitations should go out roughly two months before the wedding, with four to six weeks being the closest you should cut it. Give out-of-town guests with complicated family or work arrangements as much advance notice as you can. You can even send out save-the-date postcards six months to a year in advance, if you've managed to think that far ahead. This is particularly wise if you're planning for a holiday period, like Labor Day or the Fourth of July, for which many people make their vacation plans in advance. Airline low-fare blackouts often apply during these high-volume times, so it's thoughtful to give guests loads of time to find a good rate.

> **TIP:** *If you lack the time or the creative instincts, but still want one-of-a-kind invitations, get in touch with your local art school to find design students, budding calligraphers, and printmakers.*

Whose Name Goes Where?

Traditionally, the bride's family hosts the wedding, and so the invitation begins with "Mr. and Mrs. Empire request the honor of your presence at the marriage of their daughter, Fiona Empire, to Mr. Beauchamp King, Saturday, the first of June, at eleven o'clock," followed by the location of the ceremony and reception. Response cards are included, along with invitations to the rehearsal dinner and related events, if appropriate. But what if your family is less than traditional? Modern families being what they are, infinite variations exist on the basic structure. A good up-to-date etiquette guide will take you through the minefield of decorum that more-than-nuclear families can represent. Tradition holds that when the bride's parents are hosting the wedding, the groom's name on the invitation is preceded by his title—Mr. or Dr.—while the bride's name is not. (The opposite is true if the groom's parents are the hosts.) If you and your fiancé are hosting the wedding yourself (in that your parents may be attending, but the bills and planning are all your responsibility), then the invitation would read, "Miss Fiona Empire and Mr. Beauchamp King request the honor of your presence at their marriage . . ." or "The honor of your presence is requested at the marriage of Miss Fiona Empire and Mr. Beauchamp King . . . "

Many stationery stores offer book after book of invitation styles, fonts, and papers for you to peruse. Feel free to cruise through these to see what's available. If you decide you want something less classic, ask the graphic designers you know whether they'd be interested in designing your invitations, even if they're your professional colleagues. Many commercial designers are artists at heart and will leap at the chance to do something off-the-wall that only has to please you, not a conference room full of corporate clients.

Before you order, go back to your guest list and see how many invitations you'll need. It's a good idea to order a few extra invitations, just in case you make a mistake or two while you're addressing or assembling the invites. Couples who live together can get one joint invitation (make sure to address the envelope to both parties). If you want to emphasize that spouses or partners are included, you can write in a personal note: "Hi, Brian! We hope you and Jack can make it to our wedding," or "Hope you'll bring Caitlin along—you guys are next!" This is a nice touch if a guest has a significant other whom you don't know all that well.

RSVPs

Keep track of your guests' RSVPs. No matter what the final number is the day before, add 10 to 15 percent to accommodate last-minute guests. So if you've had 200 RSVPs, count on 220 to 230 guests. People who didn't RSVP will always show up. Conversely, people who did RSVP may not show up, but it's better to be safe than sorry.

DÉCOR

Now that you've got your space, what are you going to do with it? Depending on your style, amount of help, and budget, your décor can range from white linen and silver candelabras to picnic tables and pink balloons. If the space is already gorgeous, you can relax. Simple is usually better, in this case, especially if there's a stunning view or a beautiful natural setting. If the space is serviceable but boring, then go wild! For a night wedding, lighting is the first way to transform a space from dull to dazzling. A combination of candlelight and well-placed theatrical lights (using soft, warm gel colors like pink and amber) is the most flattering and manageable. Gobos are stencils that fit over the frame of a theatrical light, which can be used to cast evocative shadows on walls and ceilings—leaves, ferns, dots, and abstract patterns are all popular.

At one wedding we attended, the bride and groom held their ceremony in a theater. A trompe l'oeil backdrop depicting an elegant wood-paneled library with a large bay window was hung at the back of the stage. Through the window, the "sky" in the bay window (actually a scrim) slowly turned from pale blue to sunset pink, then to deep orange, and finally to the rich indigo of night, complete with glowing full moon, all thanks to a lighting design created by a friend who worked in a nearby theater. Because both the bride and groom were theater professionals, a lot of the work had been done by their theater friends as wedding presents. The ceremony was the focus of their style efforts; since they were paying for their own wedding, they held the reception at a nearby rental hall and kept it simple and easy. Guests met the night before and helped set up tables and chairs; on the day of the event, a hired team of caterers set up a buffet dinner of pasta, chicken, vegetables, and salad.

Whatever flavor of décor you choose, make sure you carefully read the terms of your location rental agreement. Some places might not allow every variation of decoration. Other places may have a strict time limit on setup and break down, and you'll want to edit your plans accordingly.

Rent or Buy?

Obviously, you're not going to buy eight dozen Champagne glasses or a hundred cake forks. If you're having a big reception and your caterer won't be providing these utensils, you'll have to find a place that will rent them to you. Party-supply rental outfits abound, and finding the one for you can be as simple as calling the listings in the phone book and collecting estimates. Find out the company's policy on breakages. You'll also want to know how those forks will be getting to you and how they'll be getting back (do they deliver, or will you have to pick them up and return them yourself?).

The smaller your party, though, the more fun it can be to collect your own decorating gear (although you'll probably still probably need to rent the glasses, flatware, and plates). Estate sales and flea markets are great places to find elegant vintage tablecloths and linens. For that country chic look, try unmatched lace, damask, or cotton tablecloths, all white. Indian sari fabrics can make beautiful tablecloths and runners, as do those Indian printed cotton bedspreads. White milk-glass vases can be found by the dozen at any thrift store. Line a long table with mismatched white vases, each filled with the same flowers but in different arrangements. Mason jars can double as vases or, with candles inside, as impromptu hurricane lamps (especially good for an outdoor evening wedding, where even a light breeze can blow out unsheltered candles).

Centerpiece Ideas

However much of a minimalist you may be, you've got to put something in the center of the tables if you're having a sit-down meal. Here are a few of our favorites:

* Groovy bamboo. Make a jagged column out of different lengths of bamboo, tied together at the base. Stand the bamboo column in the center of a clear bowl filled with water. Add small floating votive candles and gardenia blossoms.
* Gothic glamour. Collect mismatched candelabras. Adorn with chandelier glass and brilliant-colored beads. Swath base in velvet. Use extra-long tapers to keep flames far away from fabric.
* Sea anemone. Fill large, round glass fish bowls with blue and green glass beads, sea glass, faux pearls, and shells. Cover with water and float votive candles on top.

- Christmas treat. Wrap miniature white lights around tiny holly bushes in silver pots.
- Grand hotel. Fill assorted silver or pewter pitchers with pink and white sweetheart roses and trailing greenery.
- Wedding piñatas. Pack white piñatas (in geometric shapes like stars or pyramids) with silver dragées, Jordan almonds, foil-wrapped chocolates, paper streamers, and confetti. Place one in the middle of each table, and surround with sparkly Mylar confetti. Later, they can be attached to a long pole and batted by the bride and groom.

Or try these simple centerpiece ideas:
- Lemons and limes piled in silver or glass bowls
- Apples and ribbon-tied cinnamon-stick bundles in polished wooden bowls
- Beautiful flowering plants nestled in sterling silver or antique bone-china soup tureens, surrounded with small silver-framed family portraits
- Mismatched sterling silver candlesticks clustered together on deep jewel-toned tablecloths
- Frilled hybrid tulips leaning out of tall, white antique china pitchers

Ice Breakers

Since weddings often throw together people from all walks of your life, goofy little toys and snacks on the tables can help break the ice and make people feel welcome right from the beginning. Everyone loves to play with gummy rubber monster finger puppets and plastic hula girls. You can scoop these up by the handful at your local kitsch emporium (and, while you're at it, get some nostalgia-inducing candy like BB Bats or Mary Janes). One of our favorite conversation-starters is to scatter framed pictures from other family weddings around the tables. Cousins, grandparents, siblings, parents . . . round up their old photographs any way you can. What a surprise it would be for people to revisit their own weddings! On second thought, since 50 percent of American marriages now end in divorce, this could open up an entirely different can of family worms. Whatever—if your extended family can handle it, go for it!

Programs

Putting a program on the seat of each chair may make you feel like you're hosting a high-school graduation. But besides tipping off guests as to the order of events, a well-worded program can help express the feeling of your wedding. Usually, a basic program lists the different "stages" of the wedding, for example, the entrance of the wedding party, minister's welcome, invocation of the four directions, appeals to the Great Spirit, exchange of rings—whatever's going to be in your particular ceremony. Programs add a personal touch and they're nice souvenirs for people who like that sort of thing, but they're not wholly necessary, especially if your ceremony is a brief and/or casual one.

Favors

Just because you eschew the packets of inscribed Jordan almonds doesn't mean you have to forego all favors. Some favors we like include tiny potted plants—guests can take them home and plant them in their gardens. Handfuls of sweets in colorful cellophane bags tied with ribbons make perfect favors and they dress up the tables, too. Music lovers might want to make a special tape or CD featuring songs from the wedding for their guests. As with any element of your wedding, tying the favor into the theme of your wedding, or to the interests you share as a couple, will make the favor seem that much more special.

TIP: *If you're having your wedding outdoors on a sunny day, provide a stack of Chinese paper parasols for the wedding party and guests. Besides offering shade and looking festive (in that very Gatsby-lawn-party way), they are sold for just a few dollars each in most Asian shopping districts.*

FOOD AND DRINK

How you approach the food and drink at your wedding will be determined in part by your location and by your guest list. At a formal wedding, drinks are typically served before the ceremony (for the early birds), and drinks and hors d'oeuvres are usually offered between the ceremony and the main meal. Of course, all this sipping and noshing adds up and, frankly, we think formal sit-down wedding dinners have the potential to be pretty deadly. The bride and groom are sequestered with their families at a head table, everyone else ends up making desultory small talk about real estate and the weather, and the food is usually forgettable at best. Still, if you have your heart set on a sit-down dinner, you should know that you have essentially two options: the buffet and the full-service meal.

At the ever-popular buffet, guests line up, usually in order of table, beginning with the head table. Buffet-style meals keep the costs down, because you aren't paying for a lot of food servers. The downside is that guests may still be waiting their turn in the buffet line when the folks at the head table have gobbled up the last of their food and are ready for a turn on the dance floor. A full-service dinner—meaning a dinner where a staff serves the entire party at once—can be a very expensive affair, but it ensures that everyone eats at basically the same time.

If you're having an intimate wedding, your food and drink options are greater. You can get friends and family to help assemble a truly delicious home-cooked meal. Mix up a big batch of sangria and order a keg of good beer, and you're done. At a small wedding, a buffet doesn't present the flow problem nearly as much as at a larger wedding. And, if yours is to be an intimate affair, a high quality, catered sit-down meal or fixed-price dinner at a good restaurant may be affordable to you.

Regardless of your wedding size, the location you choose may impose some food and drink restrictions. Some places require that you choose from a list of preferred caterers. Some places have no kitchen facilities and will require that all food be prepared off site. Research your options before settling on your menu.

Cocktails and Hors d'Oeuvres

If having everyone sit down together around dinner tables is not your first priority, we recommend our favorite food-and-drink option: the cocktail party. At cocktail parties, everyone's mobile. People move around like molecules, bouncing up against each other, creating energy and infusing fun into the event. Serving a generous array of hors d'oeuvres is a way to give people food without all the fuss of seating cards and table settings—not to mention the price of a full-on meal.

A buffet selection of bite-sized snacks makes the easiest hors d'oeuvres party. You'll have to provide plates, napkins, and forks, but you'll save on labor costs, since you won't have to hire servers to circulate through the party. To keep a buffet looking fresh, don't put all the food out at once. No one wants to eat from a nearly empty, picked-over platter. Instead, use smaller platters and replace them with full ones as soon as they start looking skimpy. Make sure that the area around the buffet stays tidy; don't let it get too littered with squashed napkins, used forks, and half-eaten miniature quiches. If you don't have servers on hand, be sure to appoint a few people to keep tabs on the food tables and keep things regularly refreshed.

Passed hors d'oeuvres, while more expensive, are more fun for your guests, since they don't have to queue up to get fed. Instead, the sushi, the dim sum, and the slivers of onion-and-pancetta pizza come right to them, without their having to miss a word of a good conversation or find a place to put down their drinks. You may want to do a combination of the two, offering a big basic buffet of cold foods and passing trays of hot cocktail snacks.

Carolyn had three receptions for her wedding: a cocktail party for her San Francisco friends followed a week later by a larger party at her parents' house in Washington, D.C., and the next week, a reception in Paris given by Laurent's family. For the first party, she and a friend took a trip to a local gourmet grocery and stocked up on crackers, cheese, patés, crudites and fresh fruit, boxes of tiny cookies, and a ten-pound box of assorted chocolates. Dozens of *olivetti* (bruschetta topped with crushed olives and herbs), a huge bowl of pasta salad, and a blue-cheese-sherry-bacon dip rounded out the snacks. Five trays of finger sandwiches from a deli filled in the corners. When the cocktail party was over, they packed up the remains and had an after-party at a friend's house.

For the D.C. party, Carolyn's parents hired a caterer, who provided high-end treats without the stiffness of a sit-down meal. As Carolyn recounts, "The cost was a fraction of renting a restaurant or inn. I wanted the wedding at home, and didn't want a fuss. They wanted something nice. This was a great compromise."

On the menu:
- Miniature buttermilk biscuits with ham
- Buffalo wings with blue-cheese dressing
- Fruit and veggie platters
- Miniature beef Wellingtons
- Salmon on potato wedges with sour cream and caviar
- Crab puffs
- Crab Cakes
- Miniature egg rolls

Three roving waiters and one dedicated bartender ensured that she and her parents were able to relax and have a wonderful time without worrying about anything. The staff also schlepped all the plates and glasses, cleaned up, and even vacuumed. "The next day, we all relaxed around the fire with the delish leftovers, drank wine, and watched the Redskins game. Heaven!" says Carolyn.

If you're serving something very perishable, like sushi or raw oysters, having adequate refrigerator space and prep room is essential. A nearby hand-washing sink is also a necessity, so that servers and cooks can wash up frequently even if the main sink's stacked with used pots and pans.

The French party featured paté, Champagne, and a view of the Eiffel Tower.

TIP: *If you're planning a party that will go on into the wee hours, make arrangements for a scrambled-eggs-and-Champagne breakfast (with plenty of piping-hot black coffee) to be served around three in the morning.*

Here are a couple of cocktail-party menus you might consider:

Easy Glamour

- Spiral-cut ham
- Huge mounds of peeled, ready-to-eat shrimp
- Long-stemmed strawberries
- Chocolate truffles

Fancy Glamour

- Made-to-order sushi
- Mixed satays (skewered cubes of marinated and grilled chicken, tofu, and pork) with assorted dipping sauces
- Skinny wedges of exotic pizzas
- Bite-sized fresh fruit tarts
- Molded chocolate swan boats filled with vanilla ice cream and fresh berries

Drinks

Instead of a full bar, the libations at weddings these days are often limited to soft drinks, beer, red and white wine, plus one fabulous specialty cocktail. Designate one bartender to be the cocktail mixer (make sure to have some great cocktail shakers on hand!). Pick a drink with plenty of mixer in it (as opposed to, say, martinis) so that your guests don't get too crocked too fast. Punch bowls—complete with floating ice rings studded with cherries, mint sprigs, or pineapple cubes—are also making a comeback, both with and without alcohol. (Make certain it's clearly labeled, so sober guests won't worry and the teenagers will know which one to sneak sips of.) A sophisticated, nonalcoholic punch is a festive alternative for younger and/or non-drinking guests. For a punch with *punch*, use fresh fruit juices and lightly sweetened mixers like club soda or ginger ale—stay away from the Kool-Aid! No cheapo liquors (wicked hangovers) and *no Everclear* (unless you really want to see your bridesmaids dancing topless on the bar). To pick some special cocktails, cuddle up with a good cocktail recipe book and pick a few that sound fun. Try them out first to make sure you like the way they taste. Here are a few of our seasonal favorites:

Spring/Summer Quenchers
- Pimm's Cup
- Margarita
- Mai Tai
- Tom Collins
- Mojito

Fall/Winter Sippers
- Sidecar
- Apple Pie
- Singapore Sling
- Cosmopolitan
- Sazerac

Brunch Drinks
- Ramos Fizz
- Bloody Mary
- Mimosa
- Sangria

For a morning or early-afternoon wedding, Champagne cocktails make a classy alternative to the usual sparkling toasts. Here are a few variations on the theme:

- Kir royale (cassis and Champagne)
- Bellini (peach puree and Champagne)
- Champagne framboise (raspberry puree, Chambord liqueur, and Champagne)
- French 75 (Champagne with gin, lemon juice, and Cointreau)
- American Beauty (rose petals floating in Champagne)

Establish whether or not the bar or venue will provide the alcohol to be served, and what you're going to be charged up front. It's very likely that you'll have unopened bottles of liquor, wine, soft drinks, or mixers left over at the end of the night; find out ahead of time whether or not these can be returned for a refund.

The Cake

Big, white, and as fluffy as air: why do so many wedding cakes taste like equal parts Crisco, sugar, and cotton balls? Since it's such a given that the wedding cake won't be tasty, many brides and, alas, many bakers, focus on the exterior, not the interior. But there's really no reason not to start from the inside and move out. Find a bakery that makes really, really delicious cakes, and see what they can do for you. Many bakeries that do a lot of wedding cakes have the whole thing down to a small set of variations: white cake with lemon filling and vanilla buttercream icing; spice cake with mocha filling and vanilla buttercream icing; lemon cake with raspberry filling . . . you get the picture. If you work one-on-one with a smaller bakery, you might get a more creative combination. Elizabeth Faulkner of San Francisco's Citizen Cake loves to do rose cakes: one of her favorites is a vanilla genoise cake, layered with buttercream that's infused with black pepper and rose petals, and scattered with organic red rose petals. Faulkner also loves to flavor her cakes in unexpected ways: chai with chocolate, for example, or apricot with lavender. Brides who come to Citizen Cake are often stunned by how good her cakes taste; they also can't believe that there are so many more flavors than just chocolate and vanilla.

Be clear about the kind of cake you want—but also know that not every baker will be able to make what you want. Most of Faulkner's cakes tend to be architectural, with the layers built up in interesting shapes like a Frank Gehry building. If a bride comes in clutching a picture of a big, swag-and-flower-decked pouf, Faulkner will prod to see if that's truly what the bride wants—some brides don't know that they can have a cake that isn't encrusted with sugar roses or sealed in fondant. If the bride is sure that a Victorian fantasy is what she really wants, Faulkner will usually suggest another baker. In our opinion, this makes for a better caterer-client relationship, since the both the bride and the baker will be working with someone who fits their style. One bride we knew really wanted a down-home, bake-sale-style devil's-food cake for her wedding. But because she was in the food business, a well-known chocolatier and pastry chef offered to make her cake. It was an offer she couldn't refuse, and of course the cake turned out to be absolutely stunning. But with its dacquoise layers, mocha filling, and chocolate-hazelnut ganache, it was much fancier and fussier than the rich, gooey American layer cake she'd really wanted. The moral? Don't be intimidated by a baker's reputation.

Ideally, your cake should be assembled where it's going to be eaten. Find out who will be coming to the site to set up your cake. If the baker will be sending one of his or her assistants, get a phone number where you can reach the baker directly in case of emergency—if they bring the wrong cake, for example, or if the cake looks very different from what you had agreed upon.

When you're mapping the layout of the reception, plan a place to display the cake. If the ceremony will be taking place outdoors in daylight, put the cake table in the shade so the icing won't start melting down the sides of the cake. If you'll be indoors, don't forget to put a lamp nearby, especially for a nighttime wedding. People will want to see you cut the cake, so don't make them squint. Wedding cakes don't come cheap. Let your cake get the admiration it deserves.

You've Got the Look

A graphic designer, Carolyn had worked with photographer Dwight Eschliman on several national magazine ad campaigns. He wasn't a wedding photographer, but he had exactly what she was looking for: a fresh eye to capture her special day, with documentary-style photographs. As she describes it, she wanted "a cross between the Beatles' A Hard Day's Night and a 1960s Godard film." Dwight caught the bride and groom romping through San Francisco in their wedding gear—she in a 1960s-style cocktail dress and fur-collared swing coat, and he in a fitted Mao jacket and black wool slacks. Capturing the couple running up the stairs of scenic Telegraph Hill, swinging around a lamppost, posing in front of the flashing neon girls outside the Garden of Eden Pleasure Palace, Dwight created a black-and-white stop-action whirlwind of activity. The result? According to Carolyn, "the best wedding album" she has ever seen.

Point and Shoot

Sure, you could toss around a dozen disposable cameras, but you might end up with twenty pictures of your guests' feet, courtesy of your four-year-old nephew. Kristin and Colin had a better idea: they hired "The Great Keverini" to create a bit of interactive entertainment. "Keverini," also known as professional photographer Kevin Berne, arrived in costume (sweeping black cape, top hat, and mustache) and set up a photo booth surrounded by costume accessories and craft supplies. Guests dressed up, got their photos snapped, then pasted the black-and-white Polaroids into a large-format wedding album, using markers, glitter, and other fun stuff to decorate their own special page. According to Kristin, "The finished product was an amazing keepsake, and a true capturing of personalities, as well as a meaningful moment in time."

If something truly awful happens during the twenty-four hours before the wedding (we could recount a lot of scenarios here, but they'd just stress you out—take a deep breath now), send someone out to the nearest big supermarket and tell them to buy the biggest sheet cake (or cakes) they can find. Most people are perfectly happy to eat whatever sugary, cakelike item is set before them. Don't feel compelled to recount the evil ways of the bakery to everyone in the receiving line. Enjoy your wedding, serve your cake with a smile, and get restitution from the bakery *after* the wedding is over.

What if you just don't like cake or don't want a cake? Like a bouquet and a white dress, a big ol' cake is something that people expect to see at a wedding. But if you don't want it, don't feel that you have to have it. If you're having a sit-down dinner or lunch, try having a plated dessert brought out instead, whether it's crème brûlée or tiramisu. Piles of yummy cookies, brownies, or petit fours are a perfect ending to a buffet meal. For clients who don't want a typical cake, Elizabeth Faulkner has created what she calls a "landscape cake"—a three-dimensional dessert platter containing several kinds of sweets, from a sheet cake and a *croquembouche* (cream puffs stacked together in the shape of a pyramid and covered with spun sugar, a tradition at French weddings) to a mound of truffles or cookies. And if you want apple cobbler or pineapple upside-down cake, have it. If your dessert is yummy, it will make people happy.

As we mentioned in Chapter 1, making a wedding cake is best left up to the pros. However, what if you just want cake—or, to be honest, *lots* of cake—at your wedding, without all the fuss of a fancy, formal wedding cake? Here's where a potluck can be fun. Ask all the home bakers on your guest list to bring along their best cake. Arrange all the cakes on a long table, and let the guests dig in! This way, your kitchen-savvy guests get to show off, and the rest of the guests will certainly find at least one kind of dessert to love. In Cajun tradition, all of the bride's relatives whip themselves into a baking frenzy in the days before the wedding. On the big day, a designated "cake room" is filled with cakes of all shapes, styles, and sizes. The more cakes, the more happiness the newlyweds are destined to have.

Not having one big cake will also free you from the pressure to do that horrible cake-in-the-face thing—which reminds us: DON'T DO IT! Not even if every single guest yells and screams. Urging the bride and groom to smear cake on each other's faces is really, really rude and seems rooted in an assumption of hidden marital hostility, of the "Take my wife—please!" variety. Plus, it ruins your makeup! Feed each other, by all means, but no stuffing and no smearing.

Sweet Nibbles (or, What to Serve instead of Those Filling-Shattering Pink Candy Almonds)

- Truffles
- Chocolate-dipped dried or glacéed fruits (For a winter wedding, these are much better than the tasteless long-stemmed strawberries available out of season)
- Fortune cookies with *tasteful* custom-printed love-and-romance fortunes inside
- Mexican wedding cookies
- Hershey's Kisses
- Baci (hazelnut-and-chocolate candies wrapped in star-patterned silver foil with a little love poem inside, made by Italian candy company Perugina)

THE SOUND OF MUSIC

Even if you cringe at the thought of hearing "Here Comes the Bride" on your big day, music is an integral part of almost every wedding. You don't need an entire orchestra or the Vienna Boys Choir, either: there are dozens of different ways to have music at your wedding, from hiring a band for the reception to burning a custom CD of your favorite songs to swing you down the aisle. Whether you want a polka party or a groovy disco bash, we've got tips for you.

Finding a Band

First, talk to your favorite bartender at your favorite club. He or she will either be in a band or know people in bands whom he or she can recommend. No luck? Go to a local record store, brave the cooler-than-you indie-rock guys behind the counter, and ask about the local scene. Quickly make a few notes as you exit the store. Or cruise through the entertainment listings in your local alternative weekly paper. Then try calling or dropping by a club or venue that frequently features the type of music you're looking for. Ask to speak to the booker. Club bookers are regularly deluged with demo tapes, headshots, and press kits from bands dying to get a gig. Once you've convinced them that you're not a rival booker in disguise, they'll be happy to clear some of those demos off their desks. Ask for the contact info for bands they've actually worked with first; that way, you can get the skinny on these bands before you hire any of them: Did they show up on time, play a good set, and break down their equipment on time? Did they get into any fights? Abuse the bartender? Take off their pants during the show? These are things you need to know before you ask them to play your first dance. Once you get a few names, do some more investigation. If you live in a city, you probably know somebody in a band. And people in bands know other people in bands, if only by reputation. Ask around, and ask your friends to ask around. It's not foolproof, but it's a good way to get a little more information. After all, you did it after your first date with your boyfriend, didn't you?

- **All your friends in one band:** *If many of your friends are musicians, you can create a custom wedding band. At their wedding, Gina and Eric had their band play everything from Stevie Wonder to Parliament. At the wedding of band mates Jill and Owen, all their friends played short sets in honor of the bride and groom.*

- **Dueling DJs:** *Two DJs with different styles alternating beats.*

- **Eighties new-wave dance party:** *OK, we know we're dating ourselves, but if you were in high school or college during the eighties, you know that Duran Duran and A Flock of Seagulls are going to make your friends shake it. Just make sure you grab your grandma and drag her out on the dance floor when the Go-Go's start singing, "We've Got the Beat."*

- **Lounge:** *Sounds ranging from sparkly French 1960s Euro-pop to neo-cheese.*

- **Mariachi and salsa:** *Any community with a strong Latin population should have an abundance of salsa and mariachi bands. Scour Spanish language newspapers, restaurants, clubs, and churches for spots where they might play.*

- **Middle Eastern music with belly dancers:** *You'll find the bands by asking for referrals at your local belly-dancing studio. You'll find the dancers at the studio. Or go to a Middle Eastern restaurant and ask the owner to recommend some groups.*

- **Nostalgic torch sounds:** *Check out jazz clubs and hotel lounges to find local torch singers.*

- **Polka:** *You'd be surprised how much fun a bunch of guys with accordions can be. Some friends found their polka band at the neighborhood Polish church.*

- **Rockabilly:** *Twangy western guitar, Johnny Cash, Patsy Cline—what could be better?*

- **Seventies soul:** *DJs who spin 1970s soul get parties hopping faster than you can say "Funkadelic."*

- **Surf bands:** *These bands play music that's fun, frolicsome, and fierce. The obvious choice for a California beach wedding.*

Local Bands

Usually, local bands play for cheap. If they haven't gotten a record deal yet, and you didn't find their name in a wedding directory, their rates will probably be very reasonable. Look for a band with a sense of humor. Cheese is back, as are the kind of songs that would please both your irony-minded hipster friends and your mom—"Ring of Fire," "It's Not Unusual," and "What's New, Pussycat?" can be counted on to pack the dance floor. If you have any song requests, be sure to pass them along to the band in advance.

For classical music, a good place to start is a local music conservatory. Only a very small percentage of classically trained viola and oboe players make their living playing full time in a symphony. The great majority teach, play the  piano for ballet classes, and, yes, work weddings. Often, the music school will have someone in the office who handles referrals and job listings. Classical musicians can usually be counted on to show up bathed, shaved, and appropriately dressed in flowing black wide-legged pants or well-pressed tuxedos.

A few questions to ask yourself:

- Do I want music playing as guests arrive for the ceremony?
- Do I want music playing after the ceremony?
- When should the music start and end?
- After the ceremony, will the musicians move to the reception and continue playing there?
- How long will they be playing at the reception?
- If a meal is being served, will the music continue during the meal?
- Will I be responsible for feeding the band?
- Will the band be allowed to drink? If so, on whose tab?

Some questions to ask the musicians:

- Do you have another engagement scheduled the same day?
- What if you get stuck in traffic?
- Are you familiar with the pieces I want played?

- Do you each get a separate check, or could I just give the entire amount to one band member, who would then split the payment between you?
- How much of a deposit do you want, and what's your cancellation policy?
- What kind of equipment will you be bringing, and what do you need in terms of a P. A., microphones and stands, electrical outlets, chairs, music stands, lighting, and performing space?

Once you've picked your band, get a lawyer friend to draw up a basic boilerplate contract that specifies how long the band will be playing (excluding setup and breakdown time); how many minutes per hour they'll be working (forty-five minutes with a fifteen-minute break is standard); the agreed-upon price; and how they'll be paid (usually half up front and half after they finish playing for the night).

When you plan the layout of both the ceremony and the reception, make sure you figure out the best place to put the band, keeping in mind sight lines, room for the horns to swing or the drummer to thrash, and proximity to lights and electrical outlets.

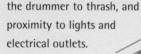

The Ceremony: How Do I Do?

When all the entertainment aspects are stripped away, the core of your wedding is the ceremony. It's no surprise that most wedding magazines and bridal guides focus on the fluffy stuff; while there's lots of advice to be given regarding choosing a dress or finding a caterer, the actual ritual of the wedding ceremony is deeply personal and needs to be defined by you and your fiancé alone.

The starting point for creating your ceremony is deciding whether you will have a religious or a civil ceremony. If you choose to have a religious ceremony, you'll probably be following a traditional format, with the vows, rituals, and blessings established by your particular temple, church, synagogue, or mosque. Most houses of worship require couples to go through a period of premarital counseling and discussions of faith; others will only marry members of their own parish or congregation. If you are planning an interfaith ceremony, you may have to do some searching to find a place that will allow, for example, a ceremony conducted by both a rabbi and a minister.

Civil ceremonies can be as simple as standing before a judge in City Hall and saying, "I do." These days, however, many couples are choosing to integrate personal aspects into their weddings, by writing their own vows or asking the wedding party to sing, play music, or read from favorite poems. You may also choose to integrate the tenets of a particular spiritual practice, like Tibetan Buddhism, into your ceremony without making it "traditional."

There are so many options available to you when it comes to your ceremony. Complete the brief questionnaire below. Have your partner complete it, too. It certainly doesn't cover the entire spectrum of options, but it's a good starting place.

Anti-Bride Ceremony Questionnaire ● ● ●

1. You consider yourself to be:
   - religious
   - not day-to-day religious, but still identified with a particular faith
   - spiritual and/or pagan
   - still scarred from years of Sunday school/Hebrew school
   - an atheist

2. In terms of your wedding ceremony, how important are the following statements? (Number the statements below from one to five, with one being most important and five being the least important.)
   - acknowledging the role of God in my life or fulfilling a spiritual practice
   - continuing the traditions I was brought up with
   - honoring the roles of family and friends in our lives
   - sharing our hopes and plans for the future
   - celebrating the love between the two of us

3. What's the most important quality the person officiating at your ceremony should have?
   - connection to a house of worship
   - personal connection to my fiancé and me
   - spiritual nature
   - charisma and stage presence

4. You've had your most important spiritual epiphanies:

- during a religious ceremony
- while meditating
- while alone out in nature
- in the company of friends

Compare your answers with those of your fiancé. A good wedding ceremony will be meaningful to both of you. Putting together the ceremony that best reflects your relationship may not be easy, but it will help ensure that your wedding is a truly personal one. It's also a good way to make sure you're on the same wavelength regarding all those deep questions, before you've sealed the deal.

Of course, your ceremony should also have lots of what makes the two of you a special and unique couple. Think about what you want to share with those in attendance. We've devised yet another little questionnaire to help you think this through.

Anti-Bride Big Moments Questionnaire

- Where did you meet your sweetheart?
- Who noticed whom first?
- How much time passed between your first meeting and your first date?
- Where was your first date?
- Where was your first kiss?
- When and how did you know that you were in love?
- When did you first get on the phone to your best friend, sister, or mom and say, "I think this guy's the one!"?
- When and where did you first say, "I love you"? When did he say it?

Some of this, naturally, is personal stuff. But why save the good stories for the toasts? Everyone loves a love story, and everyone likes to be reminded (especially if they're single) that love can strike from out of the blue. Let your guests in on a few of your secrets. If you have something sincerely beautiful to share, we promise it won't come off as hokey or cloying.

Think about how and if you want to involve friends or family in your ceremony. Their involvement could be limited to the wedding party standing up with you as you exchange your vows, or it could include speeches, poetry readings, songs, dances, and any other creative expressions. Will your parents be giving you away? Nowadays, there are many different ways to get to the altar. One we particularly like has the bride and groom entering the room from separate entrances, each with his or her entourage following behind. The bride and groom then meet and walk down the aisle together, symbolizing the shared path their lives will be taking from now on. Another woman we know walked down the aisle singing the first stanza of a favorite country-and-western song. As she reached the altar, her bride (it was a lesbian ceremony) began her walk down the aisle, joining in the song. They finished it as a duet, holding hands in front of a flowered arch. Traditionally, the groom and his groomsmen enter first, followed by flower girls and bridesmaids, the maid of honor, and finally the bride. Since the bride is usually the center of attention, this is an easy way to create suspense. By all means, follow this pattern if you wish. But don't feel bound to it. Short of doing cartwheels down the aisle, perhaps, you can choreograph your ceremony any way you want.

Guests can be involved in the ceremony even before the event. At one New Age–inspired wedding, all the women in the wedding party got together the day before to learn a song and weave a giant floral wreath to be used in the wedding. That night, the couple had a huge bonfire on the beach and all the guests performed—juggling, fire-eating, reciting poems, singing, and playing music. The next day, during the ceremony, the bride and groom stepped into the circle of flowers as the women surrounded them and sang their song.

As for writing your vows, there are lots of guidebooks out there that can help you along. Poems, religious texts, songs, essays, even love letters from famous writers can help you put into words what this wedding means to you. Anything from a Laurie Colwin novel to *Lives of the Saints*

If anyone asks you why you're an anti-bride, whip out a few of these tidbits and they'll get it. Way back when, being a bride just wasn't as fabulous as it is today.

Why all the bridesmaids?

Long ago, Romans dressed wedding attendants in the same attire as the bride to confuse any evil spirits who might try to curse or kidnap her. Bridesmaids were also employed to run interference for any interlopers, so as to make sure the bride went home in the arms of the real groom.

What's with the groomsmen?

Before man got down on one knee to pop the question, he simply absconded with a woman from an enemy tribe, a neighboring village, or a rival family. Because his actions tended to breed a certain hostility in the bride's family, the groom made sure to have his friends in attendance at the ceremony to defend him against any reprisal. Only the "best man" (or men) would do in such a situation.

Are you with the bride, or with the groom?

Centuries ago it was common for elders to give their daughters as peace offerings to enemy tribes. To prevent any unnecessary bloodshed at the nuptials, the families of the bride and groom were seated on opposite sides of the church—a tradition that holds to this day.

Crossing the threshold:

In ancient times brides were often captured and forced into unwanted marriages. Understandably, they were reluctant to enter the marriage chamber. Therefore the groom had to drag or carry her across the threshold. How this turned into the romantic sweep through the doorway that we all know now is not quite clear.

can be a source. Get out your old favorites and see what you can find. Weddings are, after all, always about the same old things: love, commitment, responsibility, a port in a storm, and a perennial Saturday-night date. Don't feel you have to reinvent the wheel or dazzle the crowd with your prose.

Many a ceremony closes with the bride and groom, along with their families, greeting guests personally in a receiving line. This is a nice, if formal, way to ensure that you meet every guest at your wedding, thank them for coming, and give each one at least a handshake or kiss on the cheek before the night is through. It's often difficult to give every person enough individual attention (do the math, it's mere minutes per guest) and a receiving line will guarantee each guest some cherished time with the couple of the evening.

There are many ways to move gracefully from the ceremony to the reception. You might choose to have a very intimate, private ceremony followed by a big, informal party in a different location. Or the ceremony might be the communal event, followed by a small dinner for family and close friends. However you choose to segue between the two, remember to appoint someone to help assist in that transition, particularly if the reception is in a different location. If there is driving involved, consider hiring a shuttle, or at least providing printed directions. You don't want guests to suffer the frustration of not knowing where to go once the bride and groom have said, "I do."

TIP: *If you're bicoastal, with family on one side of the country and friends on the other, consider two separate ceremonies, one appropriate to friends, and one appropriate to family. Then fly to the Caribbean or Hawaii and give yourself a break.*

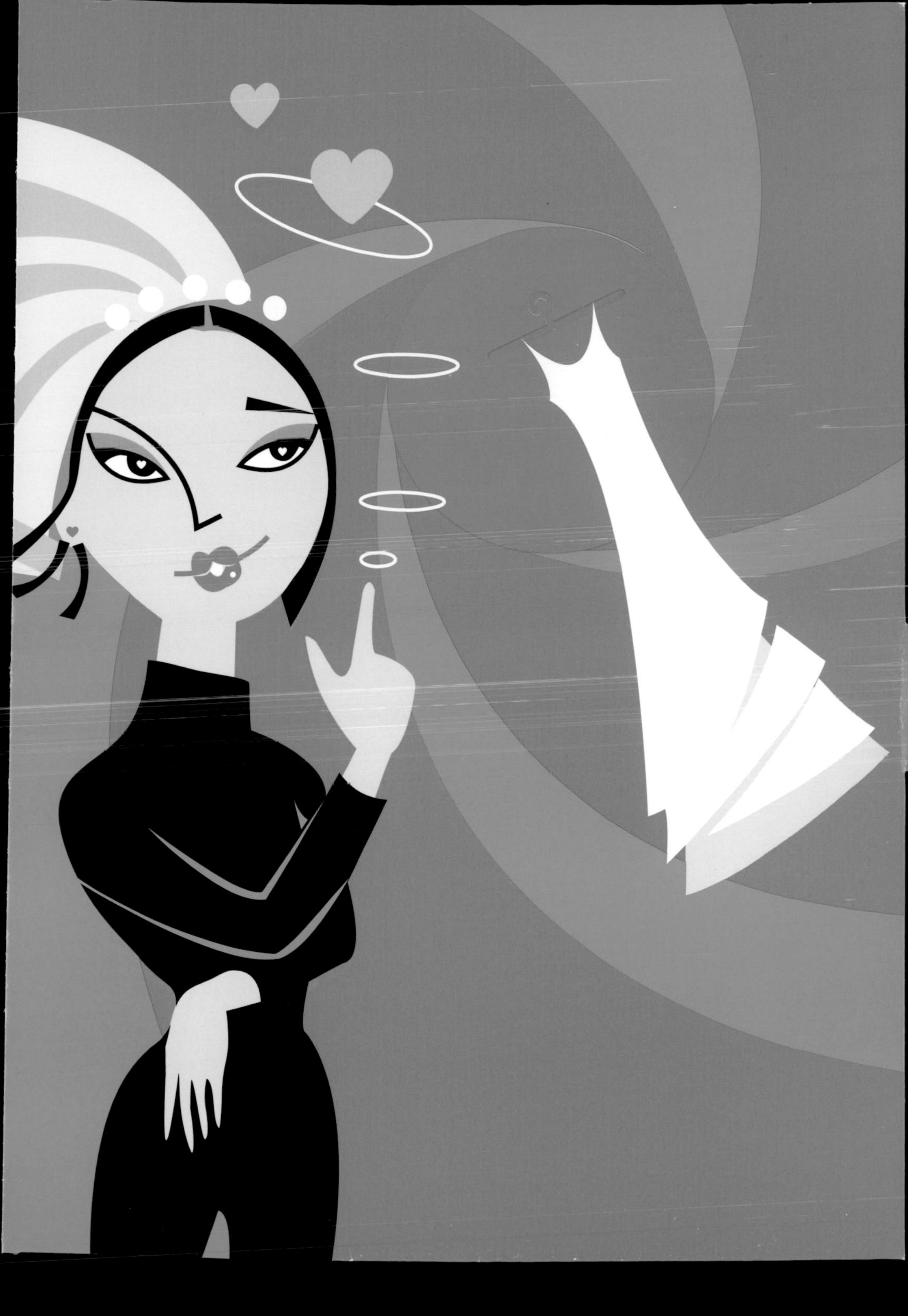

Chapter 5

The Dress: Hello, Gorgeous

Your wedding dress will be the subject of more opinions and advice than any other piece of clothing you will ever own. Everyone, from your mom to the flight attendant who notices the airport-bookstore bridal magazine stuffed into your laptop case, will feel compelled to tell you what you should wear when you walk down the aisle.

Remember, who you were last Friday night is who you'll be on your wedding day. That's not to say you should get married in a slinky tank top and a leopard-print slip (or jeans and a Radiohead T-shirt). Everyone wants to look gorgeous and special on their wedding day; it's just that it should be *your* version of gorgeous and special—no matter how much or little it resembles your mom's, your mother-in-law's, or the bridal-shop saleswoman's image of appropriate bridal wear. No matter how much of a princess you might consider yourself to be, you probably outgrew the swirly-meringue-cupcake look around the time you first started trying on prom dresses. So if you haven't worn ruffles (or pastels) since you started paying for your own clothes, there's no reason to jump into cream chiffon now. OK, there *are* reasons, but almost all of them are the result of Victorian traditions, iconic images of virginal bridal purity, and, yes, the bridal industry. Weddings gowns, and the gear that goes with them, are a multimillion-dollar industry. From the bridal-magazine ad salespeople to the satin-button wholesalers, a whole lot of people have a whole lot of money invested in the big-white-dress ideal. A fancy dress marketed as a wedding gown retails for hundreds, if not thousands, of dollars more than it would if it were sold as an ordinary fancy dress. Granted, if you want a very traditional gown, you may have trouble finding anything "wedding-y" enough outside of a regular bridal shop. However, this doesn't mean you have to look like a figurine on top of a wedding cake.

So, your first step toward getting the look you want on your wedding day is to fill out our dress questionnaire.

Anti-Bride Dress Questionnaire ● ● ●

1. When was the last time you got dressed up and felt like a knockout?

2. OK, so what were you wearing?

3. What did you see in the mirror that you loved?

4. When it comes to getting dressed to go out, your attitude is:
   - ○ Always dress like you're going somewhere better later.
   - ○ Feather boas are always appropriate.
   - ○ Yes, I can actually walk in these!
   - ○ I can wear jeans there, right?

5. What best describes your favorite clothing?
   - ○ If it's small, stretchy, and black, I'll wear it.
   - ○ a snappy skirt, a tailored shirt, and a fab little purse
   - ○ Well, I found this top at a thrift store, but I cut off the sleeves and added some fringe along the bottom, and the pants were my roommate's mom's from when she lived in Palm Beach in the 1960s . . .
   - ○ soft old jeans and the perfect faded T-shirt
   - ○ vintage cardigan, mod pencil skirt, and mules

6. My bod rules! Or, at least, this part does (go ahead and brag—no one's looking):
   - ○ my curves, curves, curves
   - ○ my killer legs
   - ○ my sexy posterior
   - ○ my beautiful arms and hands
   - ○ my pretty neck and shoulders

Thinking about your personal style can also help you figure out just what kind of wedding you really want to have. A backyard tiki party where you can wear gardenias and a sexy sarong? A sunset beach ceremony where you can say your vows barefoot in a sundress? An intimate family-and-friends affair with harps and votive candles? Also, think of what you're going to be doing in your dress. Waltzing genteelly across polished parquet? Boogying 'til dawn? Climbing down a long flight of stairs to the beach? As a general rule of thumb, daytime weddings are usually less formal than evening ones, and it's usually easier to have a less-formal wedding in summer rather than winter.

> **TIP:** *Why not have the best of both worlds? Try a traditional white dress for the ceremony, then change into a chic black cocktail dress for the reception.*

Happily, very few of us get married in bikinis, even in July. A dress is one of the most forgiving items of clothing a woman can wear; it can be shaped to accentuate the good parts and hide the less-than-good parts in millions of different ways. That said, you can drive yourself crazy trying to make your dress "fix" every perceived flaw in your figure. Look back at that questionnaire. What did you answer to question number 6? Fabulous curves? Toned legs? An awesome butt? Deliciously smooth skin? Elegant neck? Keep in mind what your fiancé loves about the way you look, too. Is he crazy about your long, tumbling, curly hair? Does he love it when you ditch the oversize T-shirts and get into something that shows off your curves? Does he appreciate your down-to-earth, tomboy style, or is he crazy about your collection of cleavage-pumping vintage cocktail dresses? Jot down in a notebook (preferably one with pockets) what elements you want to emphasize; also note the things you must or cannot have, for example, no long sleeves, no sequins, or no skinny straps. Now, start doodling. Scribble, sketch, tear out pictures from magazines. Circle what you like, rip off what you hate, and tape it all into your notebook.

Whatever your figure, you can find (or create) a dress that shows it off. A petite woman can wear dainty details like delicate crystal beading or embroidery that would get lost on a bigger gown. Remember to keep it all in proportion, however; you don't want get overwhelmed by a fussy, overdecorated dress. And no matter how tall you are, the fuller your figure is, the more you'll want some shape (and structure) to your dress. This is the time to be honest about your size. You're going to have enough to worry about—going on a baby-carrots diet to fit into a dress that's one size too small will just make you mean and cranky (you'll probably drop a few pounds just from stress anyway). Don't sweat it. Your partner loves you as you are; anyone else can take a hike. Also, don't get hung up on numbers: wedding dresses are traditionally sized small, so don't be horribly alarmed if the saleswoman in the salon tells you your gown will be a size ten when you usually wear an eight.

As for all those gorgeous magazine photos: if you've ever been at a professional photo shoot, you'd have seen that the real stars are the savvy stylists who wield glue guns, clothespins, safety pins, and rolls of duct tape in their quest to make every dress look like a million bucks. Don't become a slave to The Dress; it's there to make you look good, not the other way around.

> **TIP:** *More and more gown manufacturers are realizing that there are significant numbers of fashion-conscious plus-size women out there. To avoid any embarrassment when dealing with unenlightened salespeople, call around to bridal salons in your area and ask straight out if they carry gowns in your size. Check out our Resource Guide on page 138 for some suggestions, including Internet resources.*

Trains come in numerous lengths, from simple mermaid-type tails to the vast spans usually reserved for major European royalty. What you'll lose in mobility, you'll definitely gain in glamour. However, if you choose a dress with a train, make sure you (and, more importantly, your maid of honor) are given a lesson in train management. Some trains are attached with tiny hooks and can simply be detached, others are bundled up in a bustle, and still others can be swept around by means of a loop around your wrist. Go through the motions several times, and memorize any particularly tricky maneuvers before you leave the shop. And remember the advice of one well-trained bride: "Sometimes, you just have to nudge the guy next to you and say, 'Hey, hunk, get off my train!'"

> **TIP:** *Says Iris Hough, a senior designer at Urban Outfitters, "I found my dress—an ivory crushed-satin dress with spaghetti straps—at Daffy's for $36. A friend fitted it for me and did some alterations. The really funny part is that my gift to my husband-to-be was a pair of white silk designer pants that I found in Paris, which he wore for the ceremony. I didn't tell him until months after the wedding that his pants cost more than ten times as much as my dress!"*

Pardon me, I Speak Gown

To get what you want, you have to know some basic terminology, so here's our quickie guide to dress lingo.

Dresses

Bias cut: *Fabric is cut on the diagonal so it hugs curves. This cut is often used in slip dresses.*

  Pro: *Verrrry sexy, in a 1930s-siren, slinky-negligee kind of way.*

  Con: *You can't wear much of anything under a bias-cut dress—even a bra can show through. Also, there's a fine line between looking slinky and looking like you forgot to put on a dress over your slip.*

Basque waist: *This fitted style shows off your waist. The hem of the bodice comes to a point at the front of the belly—think Disney's Snow White. The skirt is usually full.*

  Pro: *Adds structure, especially for a fuller figure.*

  Con: *Full skirt can pouf out around the hips.*

Empire waist: *Named for Empress Josephine, Napoleon's wife, an Empire waist is gathered just under the bust, then falls in a slight A-line shape to the hem. If the hem is above your knees, this kind of dress is often called a "baby doll."*

  Pro: *Flattering to any figure.*

  Con: *Because Empire-waist dresses are so good at hiding your stomach, some guests may assume you're already pregnant.*

Mermaid: *A gown that's fitted through the bodice, hips, and thighs, swelling out into a skirt-shaped "bell" around the knees.*

  Pro: *Shows off a curvy figure.*

  Con: *No room for any lumps or bumps. Best on an hourglass figure.*

Princess cut: *Seams or darts shape the bodice into a graceful hourglass shape from bust to hips, without the usual gathered waist.*

  Pro: *Doesn't chop you in half at the waist; good for a curvy figure.*

  Con: *Can look old-fashioned; heavy fabrics (like velvet) can look bulky.*

Necklines

Boat or bateau neckline: *Usually a straight line across the collarbone from shoulder to shoulder; often paired with a fitted bodice.*

> Pro: *Emphasizes broad shoulders (in a good way); gives a tailored look. A good choice if you want to play down a big bust.*

> Con: *Bra straps can show, so you'll probably want to wear a strapless bra or merry widow with this one.*

Halter top: *Think 1950s-style bathing suit. Straps hug the neck and tie, fasten, or loop at the nape.*

> Pro: *Cool and fashionable; great with a smaller bust.*

> Con: *Shows off the upper back, so you'll need to wear a backless bra; you'll also want to make certain your shoulders and upper arms are display-worthy.*

Jewel neckline: *A simple round neckline that arcs just under the collarbone.*

> Pro: *Classic and flattering to just about any figure.*

> Con: *Not hugely exciting.*

Portrait neckline: *A deep, wide scoop neck that usually bares some of the shoulder and is surrounded by a folded-down collar or pleat of fabric.*

> Pro: *Makes your cleavage look dreamy.*

> Con: *Looks best if you have some cleavage to work with.*

Sweetheart neckline: *Think of the top of a heart shape.*

> Pro: *1950s-cute.*

> Con: *1950s-cute. Also not for the cleavage-impaired.*

Sleeves

Cap sleeves: *A small, rounded sleeve that covers the top of the shoulder.*

> Pro: *Shows off your arms.*

> Con: *Not the right choice if you're self-conscious about showing off your arms.*

Short or T-shirt sleeve: *A sleeve that comes halfway down your upper arm.*

    Pro: *A nice basic sleeve, flattering to most arms.*

    Con: *It's a T-shirt sleeve, and thus not particularly spectacular.*

Spaghetti straps: *Extra-skinny shoulder straps that hold up your dress.*

    Pro: *Dainty and sexy.*

    Con: *Can look out of proportion on a full-figured or broad-shouldered woman.*

Three-quarter-length sleeves: *A retro look—tightly fitted sleeves that end halfway down the forearm.*

    Pro: *Covers top of arms. Provides added warmth.*

    Con: *Makes long arms look longer.*

Strapless: *Dress is held up with stays in the bodice.*

    Pro: *Really shows off the chest, neck, shoulders, and arms.*

    Con: *Stays in the bodice make for a very structured dress. Also, the lack of straps and sleeves limits your range of motion when dancing.*

While white is certainly the most traditional color for wedding dresses, colorful gowns are gaining in popularity, especially for older or encore brides. If you're ready to ditch the traditional white, Wyndie Nusbaum, bridal designer, suggests a taste of the following hues:

- Tasty sorbet pastels: Pistachio, lemon, peach, champagne, lilac, green apple, ice blue
- Rich gelato colors: Cocoa brown, mulberry, pomegranate, burnt orange, deep green
- Shimmering jewel and metal tones: Ruby, emerald, gold, sapphire, silver, platinum, amethyst

TIP: *If you're planning on lots of candlelight, consider a deep-toned gown. Deep, shimmery colors can look magical in candlelight, especially if the fabric has a lot of sheen to it. Doubling up fabrics, or laying one over another, like a silver silk metal over red, offers dimension and mystery. Illusion is sexy!*

Color Matching

Just try to buy a gallon of plain white paint at the paint store. You'll be shown dozens of chips, each a little different. This one's got a hint of blue; this one's creamy; this one's peachy; this one has a touch of ochre. The same holds true for wedding gowns. You can get the white-dress effect without wearing the standard bright white. Hold up several fabric swatches against your chest and face and see what shade looks best on you.

Also, if you're shopping at a bridal salon or sample sale, keep in mind that the final dress may be significantly lighter in color than the grubby try-on one. Ask to see a swatch of the original color, or look at the color of the skirt or any other part that hasn't been handled as much as the bodice. Once you find the right shade for you, stick with it. And when you order the dress, confirm that the right color is marked on the order form.

DREAM GIRLS

Any dress you wear on your wedding day is a wedding dress. One bride we know is a Burning Man babe, computer wiz, and practicing Wiccan. No white for her! Instead, she let the woodsy, Druid-inspiring scene of her wedding be her guide. She chose a flowing, green velvet column dress topped with a green, purple, and embroidered brocade coat with wide bell sleeves, all pulled together with a heavy gold rope belt. Another bride with red dreadlocks and flawless porcelain skin insisted on a deep-crimson dress with a sleeveless corset that pulled her in and pushed her out. She complemented her look with brand-new Carolina motorcycle boots. To help get you thinking outside of the big, frilly white pouf—what Carolyn calls the "dinner bell"—we asked designers Julie Slinger, Iris Hough, and Wyndie Nusbaum to create an array of fantasy wedding attire. Here are a few of the most delicious they envisioned:

Evening Winter Wedding

Dress: Full-length velvet gown trimmed with white fur

Accessories: Loops of tiny pearls over a sleek, middle-parted updo; bouquet of red roses surrounding a lit candle

Techno Gal

Dress: A very structured, angular silk dress, either very short or straight down to the ankles in a pale, metallic color

Accessories: Wire and crystal tiara; silver gloves

Garden Party

Dress: Creamy pale-yellow suit with a short three-quarter-sleeved jacket and a fitted skirt with a side or back slit

Accessories: Sassy little cocktail hat with a wispy veil; white gloves; round or cascading bouquet of daffodils, tulips, and daisies

Tropical Goddess

Think Gauguin's Tahitian paintings.

Dress: 1940s-style wrapped or shirred dress, either strapless or with a halter top, in a bright tropical print or a deep, bright color like orange, sunset red, or ocean blue

Accessories: Gardenias and pearls

For the groom: An aloha shirt and white or sand-colored drawstring pants

Christmas in the Castle

Dress: Low-cut emerald velvet gown, with long sleeves cut medieval-style into points over the hands

Accessories: Velvet choker with cameo; bouquet of poinsettias

For the groom: Velvet smoking jacket and ascot

East Meets West

Dress: Strapless gown made of layers of iridescent sari fabric: orange and red, blue and turquoise, or pink and lilac

Accessories: Gold jewelry, including lots of bangles; on the forehead, a jewel suspended from a pendant woven into the hair

Bahamas Mama

Dress: Slip dress, dip-dyed or tone-on-tone; vintage or batik sarong

Accessories: Arms wrapped with freshwater pearls and crystal drop earrings; one gardenia tucked behind ear; bare feet with henna-tattooed ankles

Corsetry in Motion

Think Gaultier all grown up.

Dress: Boned corset in fabric of choice, with full matching skirt

Accessories: Lace-up boots, big Victorian earrings of garnet and pearls; beaded cuffs or wide, beaded choker

Jackie, Oh!

Dress: Fitted silk suit

Accessories: Perfect pearl drop earrings; gold charm bracelet; sleek and sexy slingbacks

Anarchy in the U.K./Highland Fling

Dress: Full plaid silk skirt with a bejeweled kilt pin; closely fitted black leather or velvet bodice or corset

Accessories: Choker of heavy silver chain woven with pearl; black lace-up suede boots or substantial black velvet platforms; messy updo with silver chains woven through hair; bright red lipstick

Beach Belle

Dress: Red sleeveless sundress in dupioni silk with a square neck and side slits for dancing on the sand

Accessories: Rhinestone-edged sunglasses and a shimmering silk-metal organza shoulder bag (inside, strappy red sandals and red lipstick); bare feet with bright-red pedicured toenails

Carolyn took her own advice when it came to dressing for her wedding. A curvy gal with an eye for great vintage, she wore a 1960s-era fitted cocktail dress that featured a navy Chinese silk bodice embroidered with tiny fire-breathing dragons, and a black silk skirt with a layer of midnight-blue silk organza floating on top. As Carolyn notes, the combination of fabrics hid a multitude of sins, and the fitted under-skirt created a great va-va-voom structure. Over it, she wore a matching black silk swing coat lined in midnight-blue silk and adorned with glass buttons and a fur collar. Since the dress came to the knee, the shoes were very visible—and very important! (We advise buying the best and most innovative ones you can afford.) Carolyn chose black strappy sandals, worn with bare legs and accented with a deep-red toenail polish. A heavy sterling silver bracelet, also from the 1960s, drop crystal earrings, and a multistranded necklace of gray pearls completed the look.

Bond Girl

Dress: White gold or white silver mesh halter dress (with smooth, skin-colored slip or Lycra lining to hold it all in)

Accessories: Big sparkly diamond or platinum hoops; expensive strappy shoes; wrap in white velvet overlayed with silk metal; heavy gold or platinum cuff bracelet

Forties Fabuloso

Dress: Bias-cut silk dress with sweetheart neckline in deep claret or plum, gathered below the bust with a vintage starburst brooch in the center

Accessories: Perfect platforms, with peacock feathers covering the toes, or bejeweled toe clips (visit your local vintage clothing shop or check our Resource Guide on page 138)

> **TIP:** Don't limit fresh flowers to your bouquet. Add a romantic touch to a plain off-the-shoulder or scoop-necked gown by basting on a chain of rosebuds or other aromatic flowers right before the wedding. Deep-colored flowers can stain light fabrics, so stick with flowers in pale colors like pink, peach, yellow, and cream.

Bridal Salons

OK, so you're bursting with great ideas now. Where do you start? If you want to see what's out there in the bridal shops, remember that many shops work by appointment only. A few phone calls can save you a lot of wasted effort. Make sure to bring dress-appropriate accessories—a strapless bra if you're thinking about strapless or skinny-strap styles, and a pair of heels in a comfortable height (so you'll be able to tell what dresses look good at the heel height you're used to)—and wear undergarments you won't mind every salesperson in the store seeing. But most important of all, bring a friend. Not that glamorous pal who always buys six outfits to your one, because everything just looks so perfect on her. No matter how good her taste, this is your shopping spree, and you don't want it upstaged. The shopping pal you want is the one who knows your favorite lipstick color, who bought you your favorite black sweater, who can keep you from blowing a week's pay on a lime-green couture handbag.

Bring your notebook. Let the salespeople know your wedding date and what kind of wedding you're planning: formal, semiformal, informal, daytime, evening. Most importantly, be clear about your personal style, and what you will and won't consider. Unlike regular stores, bridal stores are usually stocked with sample dresses. When you find one you like, the salesperson will take your measurements, figure out what alterations you will need (or want), and put in the order for your dress. Before you put any money down, get the crucial stuff in writing. How much of a deposit does the shop require? How many fittings will they do? Is there a charge for additional alterations or fittings? When will the dress be delivered? As with any big purchase, find out information about the shop you're buying from. Ask around and see what kind of reputation the place has. Check with the Better Business Bureau and see if anyone's ever filed a complaint. All this may make you want to get married barefoot in a sarong, but trust us: knowing the terms of this relationship before you've put down a thousand-dollar deposit will save you a lot of grief in the future.

> **TIP:** *Lipstick should stay on your lips, not on your gown! If your makeup artist can't provide a "makeup veil" to drape over your head as you put on your dress, use a pillowcase.*

One and Only: Having a Dress Made

You've got to be very, very bossy if you want your dress made. And you've got to be very articulate and very precise about what you do and don't want. In fact, in talking to a lot of recent brides, we were surprised at the number of brides who weren't happy with their custom-made gowns. Their dissatisfaction was, in part, a result of their expectations of utter perfection; naturally, since the dress was being made for them, each bride imagined that it would be *the* dress. Many of these brides had found their seamstresses through word of mouth, some ending up with inexperienced costume designers from the local theater company or recent fashion-school grads. Take our advice: Make sure your seamstress is a pro, with plenty of wedding-dress (or at least formal-wear) experience. Everyone has to learn from her mistakes; however, your dress shouldn't be someone else's learning experience.

Don't worry about what kind of wedding dress the seamstress wants you to have. Your seamstress probably has her own ideas about what a bride should look like, and those ideas may end up coming through in your dress if you don't make your wishes known. Be as clear and direct as you can about what you do want, and don't let her talk you into something you don't want.

Be honest about how you feel about the dress throughout the entire process, even if you end up contradicting your original statements. When the seamstress looks at your dress, maybe she sees the low-cut scoop neck you asked for. But when you look at yourself in the mirror, you might feel like a slutty cheerleader—not the image you want captured by every family member's Nikon.

Bridal designer Wyndie Nusbaum recommends that brides be realistic about their "real body," not the idealized body they would like to have. Know thyself, she says, and you're on your way to a dress you will love and that will love you.

Wyndie takes the "tough love" approach when dealing with a bride for the first time. The measuring tape doesn't lie, so neither does she. Using her portfolio of bridal gowns made for women of many shapes, styles, sizes, and ages, she tries to guide brides toward alternative, more flattering styles if their first choices won't work.

Wyndie also tries to get brides to be realistic about how much their weight and body size will fluctuate during the course of the dress construction. Some brides are convinced they will drop two sizes by the time the wedding comes around. One bride was upset because, at her final fitting, her dress didn't fit anymore. What she hadn't told Wyndie was that by the time of the wedding, she would be four months pregnant! Another bride came in for a final fitting, only to find her dress much too snug in the bodice. The reason? She'd had a boob job after the initial measurements were taken and had never stopped in to have her new bust measured. What we're trying to convey is that, most likely, the size you are now is the size you'll be later. However, if you're planning a serious size-changing event, whether it's body building, pregnancy, or surgery, let your seamstress in on that fact right at the start. Before the dress is begun, she can always factor in more material. But once the fabric is cut, nothing short of a resewn bodice will get a set of 38Ds into a 36B-sized top.

Before you hire a seamstress, ask for references, and see if you can talk to several of her previous clients. Getting a written contract is particularly important if she's a friend, or the friend of a friend. It's sad but true: mixing friendship with a client/provider relationship can get really, really messy. Avoid a lot of stress down the road by being clear and direct from the very beginning. Once you hire her, you'll be paying for fabric and time. Set a price limit, but don't assume that she can work miracles; high-quality fabric like *peau de soie* can run $30 to $50 a yard, and you'll probably need at least eight to ten yards for a full-length dress. Get everything in writing before you start, and especially before you buy the fabric, because once it's cut, it's yours. Ask the following questions: What is the seamstress's hourly rate? What's her estimate of the total time it will take to make the dress? How many fittings are included? When will the dress be delivered? What if you want vintage rose-crystal buttons, for example, instead of the usual satin-covered variety? What provisions will she make for alterations and revisions to the original design?

You can buy the fabric yourself, after a consultation with your seamstress, or you can ask her to buy it for you. If she buys it for you, you will benefit from her vendor discounts, generally 30 percent less than the price at your local fabric store. In addition, certain fabrics are made available only "to the trade," which means your seamstress has access to fabrics you would never see at the fabric store. Make use of her connections, and if she doesn't show you exactly what you want, ask her to get samples that match up with your ideas. Bring in paint chips, a swatch of handmade paper from an art-supply store, a photo of a cerulean-blue celadon sky—anything to make it easier for her to get inside your head. As a result, the final product will probably be a whole lot closer to what you're envisioning.

Off the Rack

Warehouse and Sample Sales

Bridal manufacturing houses usually have annual sample sales to get rid of outdated stock. Gown-seeking brides (and their mothers) can be viciously competitive, and a lot of the gowns at these sales are the kind of puffy, sequined things that would make you look like an understudy for a road show of *Tony n' Tina's Wedding*. Don't succumb to label frenzy; just because it's a Vera Wang at 60 percent off doesn't necessarily mean it looks good on you. But if you want a traditional gown, and you can fit into a standard size six or eight (some size fours and tens may also be available), you could end up getting a gown at a very nice discount. Make sure to inspect it for lipstick smudges and makeup stains before you buy, and remember to factor in the cost of getting it dry-cleaned before you wear it on your wedding day.

Something Old: Going Vintage

These days, not very many women inherit their mother's wedding dress. Even if your mom still has her dress packed away somewhere, it's very likely that the fit or the style won't be right, or it just might creep you out too much to "become" your mother to that extent. But if you've got a taste for vintage clothing and you're willing to search, you can find beautiful dresses from previous decades, often at a fraction of the price of new gowns. And, since most wedding dresses are worn only once, wear and tear is usually minimal. Here are some of our recommendations for going vintage:

Update your vintage look with contemporary touches.
Unless you and your fiancé really live a round-the-clock vintage lifestyle (and you Deco belles and rockabilly queens know who you are), you'd be wise to pair your vintage clothing with modern accessories. As cool as Grace Kelly or Jackie O. looked at their weddings, you

probably don't really want to wear a costume to yours. The older you get, the trickier it can be to look great in a full-on vintage look. A 1950s tiara on a twenty-something bride in a kooky vintage cocktail dress and boots can be charming. On a thirty-something bride, the same ensemble can look, well, silly.

Creating a vintage look when you're over thirty takes restraint and intelligence. When Julie Slinger was considering a tropical-themed wedding, she looked for a swath of vintage silk (dark purple and green swirls or cabbage roses on a dark field) to make a figure-flattering, hip-hugging, South-Pacific-glamour-girl sarong. A gardenia behind her ear; long, dangly earrings; chunky glass-bead bracelets; and vintage platforms completed the look. On her classic curvy, 1940s-gal figure, the draping fabric accentuated her considerable assets while allowing her to move comfortably throughout the day. No draggin' train or unmanageable skirts for her.

Cameron Silver, of Decades in Los Angeles, who provides vintage fashion ideas to *Vogue, Elle,* and *InStyle* magazines and works with stars like Winona Ryder, Mena Suvari, and Gina Gershon, takes a different approach. Take one or two innovation points—shoes, necklace, beaded bodice, or dress—and build your look around them, he says. Get too many things going on at once, and you'll end up with confusion. Don't let your look have "too many looks." Got a great 1960s pink chiffon halter dress? Try it with sleek platinum accessories. Or find a 1970s silk shift hand-painted in gold and pair it with strappy sandals. If you are wearing a 1940s bias-cut cocktail dress, match it with complementary but contemporary shoes. Got a pair of amazing bejeweled 1940s platforms? Wear a simple column dress and drop earrings.

It's best to keep it simple. Trendy becomes dated quickly, while wedding photos are forever. Look back at your prom pictures—do you wish now that you'd thought twice about that fringy leather skirt?

TIP: *To turn that vintage bias-cut charmeuse slip into a wedding-worthy dress, get it lined so that underwear—and nipples—don't show through.*

Make sure your vintage dress is up to the task.

Sometimes thread wears out before fabric does, and you don't want to find this out in the middle of your first dance. Take a very careful look for gaps in the seams or other signs of strain, and get them fixed by a seamstress right away.

Have a good seamstress rework or copy your vintage dress.

Vintage wedding dresses often have great detailing: a fabulous beaded bodice, a beautiful lace skirt, yards of gorgeous fabric in the train. Once you buy the dress, you can take the good stuff and create a new dress around it. Add a slim column skirt to that beaded bodice; pair an ivory cashmere shell with that lacy skirt. Or, if you love the style but hate the fabric (or if there are unfixable stains or tears), take the dress to a seamstress and have her use it as a pattern to create a new dress.

Revive antique fabrics.

Unless a vintage wedding dress has been kept very carefully over the years, it's very likely that what was once white may be closer to yellow now. Bleaching and other usual whitening methods are often too harsh for old, delicate fabrics. You'll have more success evening out the tone of the fabric with organic methods like tea dying. Dipping your gown in a weak solution of black tea can turn it a lovely, pale sepia tone. Different kinds of tea can give you different colors; experiment on an old white sheet or T-shirt until you find a shade you like.

> **TIP:** *While leather, brocade, and velvet can feel very luxurious to your hand, the thickness of these fabrics can be overwhelming in a full-length dress. To keep from looking as if you've just finished your shift at the Renaissance Pleasure Faire, try using one of these fabrics just in the bodice of your dress, with a lighter fabric in the skirt.*

How should you start your search? Call a vintage store you like, and ask whether they ever carry wedding gowns or dressy formal wear from the period in which you're interested. If they don't, see if they can recommend another shop in your area. Many urban areas have yearly vintage fairs, where a whole bunch of dealers come together to offer their wares. Here's the trick to shopping at these kinds of shows: wear something stretchy and form-fitting under your clothes, like leggings and a sports bra, so you can strip down easily instead of having

Duchesse satin: *A thick matte silk with a heavy, creamy texture. Good for elegant, flowing styles.*

Dupioni silk: *A stiff, slightly ridged silk with a papery crispness and often a slight metallic sheen. Good for cocktail suits and tailored evening jackets and pants.*

Illusion: *A very fine, see-through fabric that gives the illusion of bare skin (hence the name).*

Moiré: *Silk with a whorled pattern woven into the fabric.*

Organdy: *Stiff, semi-transparent fabric, often used under a dress for filling out a full skirt.*

Peau de soie: *Literally, "skin of silk"—a very soft, slippery type of silk.*

Taffeta: *A crisp, starchy-textured, lustrous fabric, usually silk or rayon. Makes that classic fancy-dress rustling sound.*

Tulle: *Sheer silk, rayon, or nylon net—what most veils are made of.*

Velvet and brocade: *Thick, plush fabrics. Silk velvet has a very soft nap; rayon velvet has a slightly stiffer one; brocade is usually embroidered or woven with a flat pattern.*

to wait in line for a dressing room each time you need to try something on. Also see the Resource Guide on page 138 for Web sites specializing in vintage.

TIP: *Putting aside the ethics of wearing fur, fur-trimmed gowns can look sensational, and if you use a vintage fur piece you won't be supporting the current fur industry. Tone-on-tone (for example, white fur on white fabric, or black on black) can give a dress a luxurious edge without sending you over into Mrs. Claus territory. But remember: fur is best reserved for winter weddings.*

BRIDESMAIDS' DRESSES

Do you and your friends have a standing agreement to never, ever force each other into one of those horrifying bridesmaid outfits? Stephanie and her sister did; however, Stephanie admits to being a little disappointed when her sister decided on anchorwoman-red cocktail suits and tasteful black pumps, instead of puffy apricot chiffon and dyed-to-match shoes. After all, there's a lot of mileage to be gotten out of a hideous dress, especially if some of your pals have latent drag-queen aspirations. (Although, in true bridesmaid's-dress fashion, that suit is still hanging at the back of Stephanie's closet, never worn since the wedding.) We've even heard of brides who simply told their bridesmaids to haul out the most garish bridesmaid's dress they owned.

Luckily, the rule requiring bridesmaids to wear matching dresses is definitely on the outs. Stylist Julie Slinger has kept many wedding parties happy by recommending that all the bridesmaids find a vintage dress in a single color family. The trick, she has found, is to let the bridesmaids range freely through dresses from many different time periods until they find something flattering. "It's more romantic and more individual than having everyone all matchy-matchy. And there are a lot of ways to link themes besides the same dress," says Slinger. Using this approach, your friends will look like the people they really are. And you don't have to go the vintage route; just give your bridal party a general direction as to the color family—shades of coral, say, or deep blue, or lavender—and the formality of the event

Despite the old admonishment against wearing black to a wedding, many brides these days are simply asking their attendants to wear black cocktail or formal dresses—the easiest of all outfit requests, since nearly everyone has some basic black stashed away. Women who aren't comfortable in dresses can substitute dressy, wide-leg pants and a silk or velvet top. Another option is to let everyone buy the black dress of their dreams and unify them with amazing accessories (a gorgeous citrine necklace or a pearl choker, for example). Black sheaths are the ultimate in classic chic, and your bridesmaids really will wear them again. A dressy fabric, like chiffon or silk dupioni, is a good choice. Ann Taylor puts out a great black silk sheath every autumn, as do Donna Karan and Calvin Klein. And for the feet, Kenneth Cole's Unlisted line makes super dress shoes that are very easy on the wallet, usually $40 to $70.

Over There, in the Plunging Aqua Taffeta

It's not really a wedding without one guest showing up in something wildly inappropriate. Don't be embarrassed for this guest. Instead of wondering if he or she's just dropped in on the way to playing the slots in Las Vegas, look at it this way: if nothing else, this one guest will make everyone else feel much better about their own outfits.

Cameron Silver of Decades suggests thinking realistically about the sizes of the bridesmaids in your party. If you have a size two and a size twenty-two, you can't have a uniform look that will flatter both women. If everyone is under a size twelve, however, you can probably put them all in sheaths and they'll look great in almost any color.

If you're going to have mixed-gender groups on either side, a thematic dress code that applies to both men and women works best. Typical solutions might be black-tie for men and black cocktail attire for women for a formal, evening wedding, or light-colored sundresses for women and blazers and light-colored slacks for men at an informal, daytime wedding.

John Thompson, a former Banana Republic and Espirit designer, suggests taking a group of old 1960s cocktail dresses with sparkly, multicolored brocade tops (they don't have to match), removing the skirt, and sewing a more flattering bias-cut skirt to the bottom. The skirt—each in a single color, like dark blue or black—becomes the unifying factor.

Another way to unify the bridesmaids is to create a palette of beaded cashmere shawls or vintage cardigans to be worn over silky tanks or camisoles with full ball skirts or silk wrap skirts. Besides providing a great way to unify the look, luxurious shawls or fun cardigans also make great attendants' gifts.

TIP: Make sure your shoes clear the hem of your dress in front. Nothing can make you feel quite as klutzy as tripping on your own hem.

Piercings and Tattoos: Hide 'Em or Flaunt 'Em?

Is this the right moment to reveal to your family just how much skin art you've been collecting over the years? If not, long sleeves, a long skirt, and a fully covered back may need to be your top gown priorities. If you've got just one small tattoo in a visible place, you can try a heavy cover-up like Dermablend, which is used to hide scars and birthmarks. And if your family knows about your tattoos but they aren't as enthusiastic about them as you are, consider doing some photos with a scarf or shawl draped discreetly around your shoulders to hide any body art on your chest, neck, or arms.

Then again, you may really love your tattoos and want to display them. In that case, look for a simple strapless or halter-top dress to show them off. As for getting a pre-wedding tattoo with your partner, keep in mind that a new tattoo is a tender, puffy, oozy patch of skin that will feel sore and look pretty icky for several days. Consider having a private tattooing ceremony a couple of weeks before the wedding, so you can show off your new adornments without flinching every time someone grabs your arm.

As for piercings, even if you keep your nose, eyebrow, or lip rings in for the ceremony, it won't kill you to take them out for at least some of the photos, if only so that your dad can pass around pictures of his beautiful daughter without his golfing pals thinking you've got something sticking out of your nose. After all, your parents are probably going to have a hard enough time once the DJ starts up and all the guys start dancing together. Give them a little break when it comes to the photos they'll be taking back home.

There's no one foolproof way to score that perfect dress. We've heard of brides who paid to have two or even three dresses made before they were satisfied; we've also known brides who found their dream dress on eBay a week before the wedding. One amazingly relaxed bride told us that she bought her dress a few hours before her wedding. "I couldn't find anything that I liked so I figured I'd wait to find the perfect dress rather than buy something I didn't feel beautiful in. Three hours before my wedding I found The Dress. It was a vibrant royal blue, long, flowing, and graceful. It looked like something Grace Kelly or Audrey Hepburn would wear. A true classic without a hint of white, lace, or flowers." While you may not want to put that much faith in last-minute luck, it can take some of the pressure off to remember that you're dressing for someone who loves you. As one groom says, "My fiancée wanted me to go dress shopping with her but I refused, because I really wanted to wait until the actual wedding to see her in her bridal gown. When I saw her for the first time at the ceremony, it was like the clouds parted and the sun poured in: she looked that beautiful."

TIP: *Don't forget to wear something under your dress. See-through may work for Jennifer Lopez, but inadvertently going sheer on your wedding day can be really embarrassing, especially when the photos come out.*

Accessories: Sparkle Plenty

Congratulations! You've finally found the dress of your dreams. You've gotten through the toughest part. Now you can play around with the fun stuff, all the little things that dress up your look and say "bride."

VEILS AND HEADPIECES

Let's start at the top and work down. How do you feel about veils? Whether or not you're going to wear a veil will affect a lot of your other decisions, from the way you'll wear your hair to how much jewelry you'll wear around your face. Veils come in many, many styles, from wisps that just graze the bridge of your nose to full floats of tulle.

Veils (and head adornments) we love:

- Soft veils made from antique lace or thin cotton gauze cascading down the back
- Straight, simple veils trimmed at the crown with fresh flowers such as gardenias, bits of hydrangea, or delicate, starry flowers like jasmine
- Silk head wraps, or jeweled or beaded headscarves woven into dreaded or braided hairstyles
- Beaded tiaras
- Beaded wire ponytail wraps
- Jeweled headbands with combs worked into the front of an updo

Whether or not to wear a veil is a very personal choice. Some women find the whole thing to be too creepy, the bride being shielded from all eyes until her groom claims her. Others just don't feel totally bridal until they spy themselves floating inside a cloud of tulle in a bridal-shop mirror. No doubt about it: a veil is the most instantly bridal garment we know. If you're planning on wearing a very straightforward, unadorned dress, a veil can give you that extra bit of oomph. If you're crowd-shy, coming down the aisle safely hidden behind a milky wash of netting can help banish those center-of-attention jitters. A veil that cascades down your back, leaving your face free, can make a lovely frame for you and your dress, especially if it's trimmed in lace. Maybe your mom or mother-in-law will give you less grief about not wearing her dress if you promise to wear her veil. It's up to you to decide. But if you're planning a traditional wedding look and you're not sure whether you want to wear a veil, try a few on when you're trying on dresses. You might end up surprising yourself.

If you choose not to wear a veil, you can still carry a lot of decoration around your face. Jewelry designer Sage Machado is very fond of Indian-style chains encircling the forehead with a jewel dropping right between the eyes. And American brides are finally catching on to what British women have known forever: tiaras are gorgeous! You don't have to be royalty (or a prom queen) to wear one. Don't limit yourself to the typical sparkly-rhinestone versions; some contemporary tiaras we've seen have included lots of colorful or tone-on-tone beads, wires, and flowers.

Tiara ideas:

- Crystals and jewel-toned beads on tiaras
- Beaded, hand-worked wire that covers the whole head
- Wire tiaras that can be twisted into hair
- Crystals that are wired into a cap that covers whole head
- Tiaras in the form of sculptural jewelry pieces, with all kinds of different beads and fresh flowers
- Silk flowers attached to a high comb, with a veil cascading down the back

We all deserve to be a queen on our big day—we should all be able to wear a crown! But if you're afraid of looking like a Miss Universe contestant who got off at the wrong subway stop, Wyndie Nusbaum suggests wearing a French wax crown or a beaded wire headpiece interlaced with Austrian crystal and garnets. These are grown-up tiaras, without the glare of those glitzy rhinestones. Team it with a heavy Moroccan cuff bracelet and you'll be sophisticated, mysterious, and age appropriate.

Donna Davis of Forbeadin' in San Francisco creates wire and semiprecious gem headpieces that range from subtly bejeweled headbands that circle the hair to glamorous pink-tourmalin-and-pearl tiaras made of wrapped wire. She also creates ponytail wraps that can encircle a low ponytail to form a sparkling alternative to a veil.

Sparkly stuff looks especially pretty scattered over a slicked-down, glossy pixie-style coiffure. If your hair is a little longer, try kiss curls or finger waves accented with a fresh Billie Holiday–style gardenia on one side.

According to designer John Thompson, no one over the age of nineteen should wear little barrettes, especially in the Hello Kitty fashion. Sorry, Gwen Stefani! His suggestion? Use hair jewelry instead. Tiny diamonds and pearls woven through your coiffure (whether you wear it up or down) can be very chic. Stickpins and jeweled hair pins are also very hip. If you are wearing significant jewelry elsewhere, you'll want to play down your hair jewels so they don't compete.

JEWELRY

In recent years, the fashion focus has shifted from the big dress to the big jewels. It used to be all about the dress; now it's all about using a simple, classic dress as a backdrop for original jewelry. From fine jewelry shops to department stores, the number of young women buying fine jewelry for themselves is on the rise. Semiprecious stones, beaded necklaces, and more-down-to-earth (and more innovative) jewels are no longer the domain of the dowager, but of the dazzling. Out on the town, girls are sporting Y-shaped strings of tiny amethysts and jade. Aggressive-colored stones set with contrasting smaller stones are in style for rings, necklaces, and earrings. On the high end, canary diamonds, pink diamonds, rubies, emeralds, and sapphires are back in a big way. Chunky, oversize cabochon rings are all the rage. We say, bring it on. More is more! Want to be a glamour puss? Jewels will do the job, first and fastest.

Even if you're planning on being married in white, don't assume your only choices for jewelry are diamonds and pearls. In this day and age, color and design are a key part of your look. If you're wearing a white or light-colored dress, think about using colored jewelry for accent. While pearls and diamonds are safe and always lovely, offbeat choices can add punch to a traditional outfit. Lapis or turquoise can be your "something blue"; coral and amber pieces can go beautifully with antique or tea-dyed lace. Dramatic jewelry, whether it's a wide choker clasped around your neck, a cleavage-enhancing pendant, or an armful of exotic bangles, can turn a simple gown into a showstopper.

> **TIP:** *Combine your "old, new, borrowed, and blue" into one item. A beautiful, contemporary bracelet of antique blue chandelier drops, on loan from a friend, fits the bill.*

Gina, a very modern girl with a sexy style and a great backside, was searching for a vintage-inspired look done her way. Her dress, designed by Wyndie Nusbaum, had a white velvet bodice with a silk skirt draped around a very low back—a Jean Harlow look that was exactly in keeping with the personality of the bride. She used jewelry to introduce color in subtle ways—a long string of garnets around her neck and drop earrings of vintage-inspired, emerald-cut garnets with amethyst accents. A lavender chiffon shawl and lavender platform shoes completed the ensemble.

Designer Sage Machado has a jewelry-boxful of advice on what to do and how to do it. Her style is beautiful and refined, innovative and eclectic. Much of her inspiration comes from the vintage jewelry pieces she finds at estate sales and vintage expos, which she then takes apart and reconfigures to suit contemporary tastes. For the jewelry lover who wants to approach her wedding accessories creatively and with an eye for both the classic and the unexpected, Sage offers this advice:

Mix it up.
Combine strands of precious stones and pearls in a multistranded choker, with one deep-colored central drop complementing the piece.

Think harmony.
Sparkling diamonds might just be too much for that rustic gown, but a shining choker would make the perfect companion to a simple jewel-neck sheath. Work with your dress.

Re-envision grandma's pearls.
Is the strand you inherited just too Barbara Bush? Of course, you love them and you are supposed to wear them on your wedding day (says the family). But they're not quite you. Go to an antique jewelry shop and look for a gorgeous ruby amulet, a cameo, or a big black pearl pendant crowned with diamonds to add to your strand of pearls. Whatever your style, it can be a snap to make that necklace come to life.

Wear a big piece of vintage jewelry.
A glorious Victorian topaz pendant set in old hammered gold with topaz beads in the chain could be exquisite when worn with the right gown.

Check out your local bead shop.
Search out a place that has high-quality stones as well as beads. At Forbeadin' in San Francisco, owner Donna Davis sells raw garnets, topaz, rubies, and more. Bead shop owners

Scents trigger memories. On the day of your wedding, you might want to wear a fragrance that has a particular meaning for you, such as the one you were wearing on your first date, or on the day you first said, "I love you," or on the night you whispered, "Yes, yes, I want to marry you!" Consider even having a special scent mixed for your wedding, a fragrance to remember the day by, which you can wear all throughout the first year of your marriage.

often get into the business to support their own jewelry-designing habits, so talk to the owner if you want some advice on creating a custom design.

> **TIP:** *Have your local bead shop owner teach you how to make a long string with garnets and small crystals at each end. To wear, wind it around your neck twice, and tie it around back by looping one end over the other, letting the garnets play across your bare back. Very sexy!*

Be creative.

Most good jewelry boutiques know plenty of designers who can set stones, make what you want, or remake an old heirloom into a fabulous new fashion piece. And for a lot less than you think. Don't get sucked in by that cheesy "wedding jewelry" racket. Jewels are jewels. Why invest in something you won't wear again?

Gems aren't just for jewelry.

You can use beads and gems in lots of other innovative ways. Wyndie Nusbaum has been known to use gems in her dress designs. One of her favorite designs was a one-of-kind piece that resulted when she took apart an old blue topaz necklace and strung the stones along the bodice of an Empire-waist gown, further embellishing it with colored beads. Vintage beaded bags make great bridesmaids' gifts and are glorious to carry. Jet, gold, or platinum metal-mesh wrist bags are also divine. If you can't find a bag that suits you, have your seamstress whip up a little silk pouch that matches your dress, line it with colored velvet (for sturdiness), and pin an antique brooch to it.

SHOES

A lot of typical bridal shoes are stiff, cheaply made, and, let's face it, pretty ugly. In any size over six, those white satin pumps can look like a pair of cruise ships come to dock under your skirt—not exactly flattering, especially if you don't usually step out in anything but black. Instead of searching high and low for shoes you can bear, turn your favorite special-occasion shoes into wedding-fabulous slippers. Using a hot-glue gun or artist's cement, glue on sequins, beads, or feathers. After all, they only have to last one day! Says designer Julie Slinger, "I once glued peacock feathers on a pair of open sandals—the fringes lapped all over my toes. Very decadent!" Try gluing sequins around the straps—sometimes that's all it takes to dress up your shoes enough to make them wedding-ready. You can also change the color of any pair of shoes. Metallic acrylic paint stays flexible when it dries, so it won't crack, and you can "burnish" it with a soft cloth for a weathered look. Rhinestone shoe clips or dress clips from the 1930s or 1940s can dress up a pair of chunky platform sandals. Then there are always your trusty motorcycle, cowboy, or combat boots, although you have to be a special kind of girl to carry this off. Our main piece of advice for treating your tootsies? Be comfortable. A gorgeous shoe that makes you go cross-eyed with pain after half an hour is a bad, mean shoe.

TIP: *Worried about towering over your groom? Wear flats if you must, but trust us: this is your day to be beautiful. People will remember the guy by your side as a necessary part of the picture, but they will notice your look much more than they will a couple of inches between you either way. Get the shoes you love, and don't sweat it if they make you taller than him.*

STAYING WARM, KEEPING COOL

If you're planning an East Coast wedding in June, you might think that the last thing you'll be worrying about is whether you'll have cold feet (or cold arms or cold legs). But if any part of your wedding is happening outside, do make sure you've got something to snuggle into should the weather suddenly play tricks on you.

A shawl is the best option, since you can loop it around your neck like a scarf or let it flow around your arms and back and then pull it up when a breeze kicks in. Thin, whisper-soft pashmina shawls offer warmth without bulk and are available in dozens of shades from delicate pastels to deep, rich hues. And because their trendy moment passed a couple of years back, they are expensive (they are cashmere, after all) but no longer outrageous. Soft mohair or angora shawls or cardigans, color-coordinated with your dress, can give any outfit a pretty, pettable look. Wide scarves made from crushed velvet or silk-velvet burnout, with or without fringe, look gorgeous and luxurious, especially for an autumn or winter wedding. Soft plaid shawls give a cozy, Scottish-castle feel to a winter ceremony.

> **TIP:** *Worrying more about your guests wilting in the heat than shivering in the cold? You can find cheap and decorative round paper or palm-frond fans in most Asian import-export stores, along with the more typical folding fans. Putting one of these on every seat at an outdoor wedding is a nice Southern touch (and will encourage your guests to actually read their programs, instead of just fanning themselves with them).*

PUSHING IT UP, SUCKING IT IN

If you've never worn serious foundation garments before, this may not be the time to start. If your garter pops loose two minutes before you're supposed to walk down the aisle, hooking it up again had better be second nature. So unless you're used to the feeling of being squeezed in and pushed up, it's better to go with stretchy Lycra-based stuff rather than all that frilly merry-widow business. You want lingerie that works and feels

If the fabric of your dress is of the opaque variety, and you have courage to spare, we think it's fine for you to go naked under that spectacular gown. The important part is that you feel comfortable, and that you love the way you look. Whatever you choose to wear underneath is your business, but if you think you want a little support, here are a few helpful items beyond the standard bra and panty.

Body shaper: *Any number of Lycra-based items that smooth out lumps and bumps, ranging from bicycle shorts (for rounding hips and taming jiggly thighs) to "power slips," which look like those micromini dresses that everyone went clubbing in during the 1980s.*

Bustier: *Like a strapless bra, but with more support. A bustier usually hooks up at the back, and stops at the waist.*

Garter belt: *This number hails from the days before panty hose, when stockings stopped at the thighs. A garter belt hugs the waist. Straps come down from the belt and hook to the stockings. A great, sexy addition to your underclothes, but the slightly protruding hooks make this not such a good choice for wearing under a slinky bias-cut dress.*

Merry widow: *A strapless long-line bra that features underwire bra cups and light boning around the ribcage. Some merry widows stop at the waist, and others go all the way down to the hips; the longer ones usually include garter straps. Styles can vary from lacy and barely there to sturdy and retro.*

Waist nipper: *A boned and elasticized tube that goes around your waist, giving your figure a firm nudge in the hourglass direction.*

comfortable. Whatever you end up with, bring it with you to your dress fittings. A dress worn with a waist nipper and a push-up bra will fit differently than it will worn without, but first decide what's comfortable (a wedding makes for a long, long day), and then decide what makes you look your best.

Corsets

If your dress involves a real, boned, historical or fetish-style corset, remember that you can't just jump into a corset and go. An hour or two before your wedding, start by lacing it up so it's about half as snug as you'll eventually want it. Walk around. Get used to the constriction. Over the next hour, pull in the laces little by little, until the corset is as snug as you want it. Don't rush this, and allow at least fifteen minutes between each tightening.

TIP: *If you're wearing stockings and garters, make sure to put on your panties after you get your garters hooked up to the stockings. This way, you won't have to unhook everything when you dash to the ladies' room.*

Leg Lifts

Make sure you know what you're getting in that stocking package. If you're planning on wearing a merry widow or garter belt, you want to get *stockings.* Look for ones with a little Lycra in the blend to prevent sagging and wrinkling; silk stockings sound sexy, but they snag easily and don't cling to your leg like nylon ones. If you're nixing the garters but don't want to wear panty hose, look for thigh-highs or stay-ups, which come with built-in elastic or rubber grips around the tops. Get the longest stockings or stay-ups you can find; stockings that fit around the top of your leg are much more flattering and comfortable than ones that chop you right at the fleshiest part of your thigh. Control-top panty hose aren't glamorous, but they can give you the smooth, seamless look that a really slinky gown demands. Specialty lingerie stores often sell a type of hose that combines a garter belt and stocking in one, with a wide lace band that goes around your waist and four attached lace straps that connect to the stockings.

TIP: *Buy an extra pair of stockings, and make sure to bring it with you to the wedding site. This prevents big-day meltdown if the first pair rips right before you walk down the aisle.*

SPARKLE, BABY: MAKEUP

How can you make sure that you'll look like yourself (and not Tammy Faye or Kathie Lee) on your big day? As a former model and modern-day makeup mogul, Jean Danielson, one of the founders of BeneFit Cosmetics, knows glamour. But she doesn't believe that anyone needs to be "made over," especially not on her wedding day. Instead, she suggests aiming for a soft, sexy look with a finished sparkle. Whether you do your own face, put a friend to work, or hire a pro, make sure you do a couple of dry runs before the wedding so you feel totally comfortable with your look. If you trust yourself but need a little help getting beyond your typical Monday-to-Friday neutrals, ask a makeup-savvy friend over for some girl time and makeover fun. A good way to plan your look is to pick one feature and accentuate it. For most people, that feature will be lips or eyes. As Jean notes, most of your makeup will wear off halfway through the wedding, so apply your makeup with a slightly heavier hand than usual, and carry the products in your bag for touch-ups. With this in mind, don't plan a look that won't survive a little mussing.

> **TIP:** *Tweeze brows after a bath or shower, when the pores are relaxed. Always tweeze in the direction the hairs are growing, and always shape your brows from under (not above) the natural arch. Dab brows with astringent or toner afterward to reduce redness.*

Get Wet

Moisture is your best friend when it comes to wedding beauty. Get it from the inside out by drinking plenty of water during the week before your wedding. This will plump up your skin while helping to flush out toxins. Use lots of moisturizer at night followed by a moisturizing sunscreen during the day.

> **TIP:** *Honey is a great humectant. For a quick moisture mask, mix three spoonfuls of honey with one mashed ripe banana. Slather it on, and relax for ten minutes. Rinse off with warm water and pat dry.*

Picture Perfect

Dab on concealer where you need it, but don't slather it all over your face—it'll give your makeup a cakey look. Instead, use a cosmetic sponge to smooth on a good foundation over the dots of concealer.

Go light on the blush. Excitement, dancing, and the roller-coaster emotions of the day should give you plenty of natural color in your cheeks. If you do need some brightening up, try a soft-apricot or tawny shade rather than a neon pink. Don't stripe it up your cheekbones; instead, apply lightly with a soft brush to the "apples" of your cheeks.

Powder will help keep that T-zone shine at bay. However, caking on too much pressed powder can make you look embalmed. Try a nice loose powder applied with a soft brush.

> **TIP:** *Drugstore foundation colors are notoriously unreliable—what looks beige in the bottle can be scary-orange on your face. Make sure you shop for your cosmetics at a store with a good return policy. Try on all your purchases and check yourself out in natural and artificial lighting.*

Those Lips . . .

Stephanie is a lipstick junkie—she'd happily forgo all other makeup for the chance to add yet another tube of lip-smacking color to her collection. But finding a lipstick that will stay on for a whole day of kissing, eating, talking, and drinking can be tough. To make it easier, don't expect the lipstick to do the whole job by itself. Start with a lip base, like BeneFit's Lip Plump. Uses a pencil lip liner to prevent "creeping," followed by a layer of lipstick color. Finally, slick on a layer of lip sealer like BeneFit's She Laq.

Red lipstick is super-glam and looks great in photos. But be warned: it's high maintenance, and you could end up with the dreaded "Bozo face"—a big red ring of smeared lipstick around your mouth. If you aren't prepared to do constant touch-ups and fix the occasional smudge (including getting it off your teeth), go for something more neutral.

...Those Eyes

Sparkly pink or gold eye shadows look good on almost everyone, and when applied over a neutral base they will last all day. Cream shadows crease and wear off faster than powders. If you go with a cream shadow, we suggest using a powder over a cream base, since cream alone won't last a whole day. Shape your eyebrows and highlight your brow bones just below your eyebrows with white or champagne-colored shadow for movie-star oomph. As for lining your eyes, liquid eyeliner requires a steady hand and lots of practice to get a smooth, even line. Use it only if you want a highly defined, 1960s-kitten style of makeup. Water-soluble cake liner (applied with a wet brush) is a lot easier to remove (and to fix if it smudges) than all-in-one liquid liner. For tear-proof lashes, go with a good waterproof mascara. A quick trip to the salon for tinted lashes and shaped eyebrows is your shortcut to glam (it's also great to go without mascara during the honeymoon).

Shiny, Happy People

We're talking glamour-girl glow, not super-glittery club-kid glitz. Look for butter-soft sparkle creams that will impart a sexy shimmer to bare shoulders, cleavage, collarbones, and even the curve of your spine! Be sure to try them out before buying, because some gleamers can fade out or look chalky on certain skin tones. For your face, dab dots of highlight cream on each cheekbone and blend—no blush here!

Zit Busters

If you get frequent skin breakouts or acne flare-ups, take the money you've been spending on Chanel concealer and MAC foundation and see a dermatologist. There are lots of medical routes to clearer skin, from antibacterial lotions to oral antibiotics, and the prescription stuff is a lot more effective and much less irritating to the skin than over-the-counter creams. You may also want to look at your diet—we've known a lot of women who developed lactose intolerance later in life. Once many of them cut down on the dairy, their skin cleared up enormously. Being able to feel confident in your skin is the best beauty boost we know; solve your skin troubles now and you'll save yourself a lot of stress (and money) in the future.

But what if you're just worried about the sudden emergence of one of those big-day blemishes?

- Get a glycolic-acid peel two days before the wedding to tighten pores and heal minor zits. This is especially helpful if you're on the pill and your skin is acting up.
- Slather on a pure clay mask to help draw out blackheads.
- Some tricks to dry up a stubborn zit (don't tell your dermatologist, but these do sometimes work): dab on a little of *one* of the following: Crest toothpaste, Palmolive Green dishwashing liquid, or Queen Helene Mint Julep Masque.
- For a day-of-wedding zit: Don't squeeze! Instead, dab on concealer, let dry, and pat on powder. If you pick at it, it will seep and cause a volcano effect. Covering up a blotch is easy, but concealing an oozing bump is hard. Restrain yourself.

Bridesmaids' Gifts

The tradition of presenting small keepsakes to the members of the wedding party is a pretty one, and just as you're not going to make your pals wear some really weird Martian dress, there's no reason to go all froufrou and give everyone little heart-shaped picture frames. Cruise through your favorite boutiques and see what sassy accessories they've got, from glam sunglasses to the top nail polish of the moment. You can also take your inspiration from the theme of the wedding itself. For a beach wedding, find an assortment of fun woven-plastic or straw beach bags and pack them with towels, bronzing lotion, floppy hats, and cute flip-flops. You can even throw in some beach reading material—juicy celebrity tell-alls are always appropriate when you're tanning. Here are a few other ideas for gifts that can be both heartfelt and useful:

• Cute silk, straw, or beaded handbags, all filled with home-spa treats like fizzy bath balls and luscious lip balms

• Gift certificates for manicures, pedicures, or other spa treatments

• Luscious cashmere or lamb's-wool wraps in tones that go with the bridesmaids' dresses

• Jewelry for wearing to the wedding (all identical, similar in style, or suited to each bridesmaid's personal fashion sense)

• Snuggly flannel or slinky silk pajamas in a really fun print

TIP: *Intense facials right before your wedding are not advisable. Extraction (squeezing) and exfoliation can stimulate oil glands and actually encourage blemishes. Get a soothing azulene facial instead.*

Tossing the bouquet, wearing a garter (even with no stocking)? Ever wonder why brides do the things they do? Like many traditions, the roots of these and other wedding customs lie somewhere between myth, folklore, and history.

The bouquet

Hello, Madonna: in Old England, brides got the rock-star rush from departing guests, who would often tear scraps of clothing from the bride in order to take home a piece of her good fortune. So as to create a distraction (and keep their dresses intact), smart brides learned to heave their bouquets at the crowd instead.

The veil

Centuries ago, veils served dual purposes. When the groom lifted the bride's veil to seal the union with a kiss, he claimed her virginity. At the same time, the veil ensured that the groom in an arranged marriage wouldn't back out of the arrangement before the vows were said. Only after the marriage was official could he lift the veil and behold his new wife.

The garter

The tradition of removing the bride's garter originated in the 14th century, but then it was the bride who removed it and tossed it to the men. Eventually the tradition changed and the groom, presumably to protect his bride from unruly drunkards trying to remove the garter themselves, took over the responsibility. Today it's believed that the man who catches the garter will be the next to marry.

BOUQUETS

First of all, who says you have to have a bouquet? For an evening wedding, carrying a small candle flickering in a crystal bowl looks dramatic, romantic, and flattering. A single flower, either totally plain or tied with a beautiful trailing ribbon, can look sensational, especially if you're wearing a long-and-straight column or bias-cut dress.

But if you decide to carry a bouquet, *do not* think you can make it yourself. Sticking a bunch of flowers together may seem really easy, but professionals know secret tricks with wire and floral tape that truly do make all the difference, especially in terms of longevity. A bouquet that can make it through a whole day of being clutched in your damp, sweaty hands needs special treatment so it won't wilt, shrivel, or disintegrate. You can, however, choose the flowers yourself, and then have the florist in the shop put together the bouquet for you. Talk to the florist beforehand, and make sure to plan out prices and schedules well in advance. Many variations of flower shape, color, and size of blooms are available, depending on your budget and preference. Make sure your final choice matches your dress in style and "weight." A stiff, tightly arranged saucer-style bouquet could look old-fashioned against a contemporary slip dress; likewise, a loose wildflower bouquet against a tailored silk suit might look like you just ransacked the highway median on the way to the wedding.

Keep in mind how you'll be arriving at the altar; if you're planning on walking in with a parent on each arm, make sure you have a bouquet that can be tucked easily into the crook of your elbow or held in one hand.

A very formal and elaborate bouquet will usually require hand wiring, where each stem is reinforced with skinny wire and wrapped in floral tape. A more natural (but less durable) bouquet will have the stems simply wrapped in ribbon, in any number of styles from a simple spiral loop to a solid weave (which will look like someone has French-braided ribbon into the stems of the bouquet). Your bouquet can also be inserted into a pretty, narrow holder—if it's a shiny chrome holder, it will look sleek and futurist; if it's a dainty silver filigree, you'll be channeling a Victorian maiden.

As with bridesmaids' dresses, attendants' bouquets don't all have to match. At one wedding we attended, all the bouquets were round and white, but each one was made up of a different type of flower. There was a daisy bouquet, a lily bouquet, and so on. This allowed for both uniformity and individuality in the look of the bridal party.

If wrist corsages are too prom-queen for your wedding, bring personal flowers into play in other ways. Younger members of the bridal party—flower girls, junior bridesmaids—often look lovely decked out in floral wreaths. These can look good on bridesmaids, too, especially in a country or casual outdoor wedding. Tiny buds and trailing vines are more flattering than big blooms.

TIP: *Carrying a long taper instead of a bouquet may seem dramatic, but it's actually not a good idea. The wax can drip onto your hands (ouch!) and dress, and the flame could go out before you make it down the aisle.*

At the risk of sounding like a mantra tape loop, we urge you again to chill out. In the end, everyone will think you look beautiful, regardless of any fashion disaster that may take place. Primp just enough, and then go have fun. A big smile on your face is your best accessory.

The Main Event: Here, There, and Everywhere

The days leading up to your wedding can be joyful, hectic, and, above all, crazy. Often, you'll find the phone ringing again every time you put it down, and you'll be careening between embracing your inner glamour princess and feeling like the chief cat-herder on Noah's Ark. How can you keep your cool when you're running from sauna to bikini wax while worrying about who's picking up your eighty-year-old grandma at the airport? By scheduling your time in the right ways. We've divided up these frantic days into three chunks, Girl Time, Sweetie Time, and Public Time, to help you get the love and time you need from all your favorite people.

GIRL TIME

Your fiancé may be promising to love, honor, and cherish you for all the rest of his days, but when it comes right down to it, who's really been there for you over the years? That's right—your girlfriends! They're the ones who took you out for beers when that sleazy now-ex-boyfriend dumped you, the ones who told you that you were way cuter and smarter than said ex's new girlfriend, the ones who jumped up and down and screamed for you when you announced your upcoming wedding. Make sure you get plenty of time to celebrate with the most important women in your life.

Kissing the Single Years Good-bye

No, we're not suggesting you lurch from bar to bar with a veil tacked to your head, drinking White Russians out of a penis-shaped squeeze bottle. Nor would we suggest a gals' night out with the Chippendale Dancers. If you don't already have a thing for men with shaved chests gyrating to the Backstreet Boys, there's no reason to start on the night before your wedding. But marking the end of your single life with some kind of party ritual is a great idea. Here are a few of our favorites:

- Bowling (especially if you can find a place that does theme nights or rave-inspired "cyber bowling" events)
- Mini-golf

- Roller derby
- Cooking a big, fabulous meal (at someone else's house, so you won't have to worry about cleaning up in the morning)
- Swimming, if you have an ocean, lake, or private pool at your disposal (if you've got a pool, definitely initiate some all-girl skinny-dipping!)
- Going to a karaoke bar and singing both the sappiest and the raunchiest love songs on the list
- Head-to-toe spa indulgence
- Wild dancing
- Ice-skating
- A big sleepover, complete with popcorn, brownies, and lots of trashy chick flicks— anything from *Grease* to *She Devils on Wheels*
- Dinner out at your favorite restaurant, with plenty of toasts

In the Jewish tradition, the bride is required to undergo a *mikvah* (ritual bath) on the night before her wedding, symbolically washing away her former life and entering her new life clean and pure. Whatever your background, getting wet can be a wonderful way to rinse away all your cares. Indulge in any of these cleansing rituals with your best girlfriends, or by yourself:
- Getting doused under a waterfall
- Soaking in a hot tub under the stars
- Soaking in a hot spring or mineral bath
- Swimming in a lake, river, or ocean
- Indulging in a candlelit bubble bath

> **TIP:** *Get some exercise on the morning of your wedding and get the blood pumping to your face. You'll look radiant!*

Beauty Starts with a Party

Of course, girls and beauty rituals go together. Having some company during your pre-wedding manicures and pedicures will be much more fun that leafing through a three-month-old *People* magazine. Your bridesmaids will probably be planning on getting buffed and polished, too, so why not do it together? Even if you're a short-nails, no-polish kind of gal, listen to your friends when they insist that you get a manicure and pedicure before your wedding. You can get a very sheer, pale polish, or even no polish at all. Besides making you feel very pampered, having a pro do your hands (and toes) adds a finished and well-groomed accent to your big-day look. Nail polish actually takes several hours to dry completely, so make your appointment for the day before your wedding. Make sure to buy a bottle of the polish the manicurist uses so you can fill in any chips or cracks that might happen before the ceremony.

And don't forget to eat! The number-one tip we got from recent brides? Have a decent meal before the wedding starts. No matter how much care you devoted to choosing the reception menu, on the actual day of the event you will be way too busy and adrenaline-high to eat any of it. Nevertheless, you still need some nutrition to get you through a very long, exhausting day. Schedule times to eat. If you're getting ready in a hotel, room service can be a godsend (as long as you keep the ketchup away from your dress). Just going out with a few close friends for a yummy breakfast, brunch, or lunch on the big day can really help ease those jitters. To make it truly relaxing, let your maid of honor or main attendant make the plans for this one, from calling for reservations to handling how you'll all be getting there and back.

TIP: *There are many ways to get rid of unwanted hair, and at this point in your life, you've probably already found your comfort level with waxing, shaving, using depilatory creams, or having the little suckers zapped with lasers. If you're leaving for a week of Hawaiian beach-lolling right after the wedding, making an appointment for a leg-and-bikini wax is probably a very good idea. The down side is having to endure a little bit of pain during the actual procedure, and some stubble for a couple of weeks beforehand (the more hair the wax has to grab onto, the smoother the result). But afterward you'll have at least a month of hassle-free bareness.*

One week before: *Get your hair cut (and colored, if you desire); get a facial. This will give both your skin and your hair time to relax. (And if you end up hating your bangs or getting a zit from that lavender-rosemary exfoliating scrub, you'll have enough time to do pre-wedding triage.) If you color your hair, get it done professionally. You won't have any of those unavoidable back-of-the-ear smudges and cuticle stains that come from home dying.*

Two days before: *Have your body waxing and/or eyebrow shaping done. This way, you'll be smooth and soft, with enough time for any redness or bumpiness to subside before the big day.*

The day before: *Get a manicure, pedicure, and massage (and have a hot tub–soak and sauna, if you wish). Relax, relax, relax. (But make sure to get your manicure and/or pedicure after your hot tub–dunk, because chlorinated water can be hell on polish.*

TIP: *No matter how much of a DIY girl you are, never try to dye your lashes or brows at home. Hair dye is caustic stuff. Even one drop of hair dye in your eye will sting like crazy and could cause serious damage.*

The best beauty advice we can give you is also the most boring: Drink lots of water. Get plenty of sleep. Eat those fruits and veggies. Don't crash-diet or suddenly decide to go on a no-carb or all-soybean regime a month before the wedding. Get a big bottle of B vitamins with iron (these are often marketed as "stress tabs," for good reason) and take them regularly. Cut back on cigarettes, alcohol, and caffeine. Make sure to work some stress-relieving exercise into your life, whether it's Bikram yoga or boogie boarding.

TIP: *Take a tip from the porn stars: to get rid of those itchy, red razor-burn bumps along your bikini line, try a few drops of Visine.*

SWEETIE TIME

You've got the dress, the veil, the cell-phone number of the caterer, and everyone's flight numbers tacked up on the fridge. The pet-sitter's picked up the cat, the dining room's stacked with cases of Champagne, your nails are like buttah, and, thank the goddess, your chin is breakout free. What are you forgetting? Wait, who's that guy moping in front of the TV? Shouldn't he be picking out a tux or making sure the band's amps work? It's easy to get so caught up in the minutiae of the moment that you forget to pencil in quality time with your sweetie. But nothing's more important. Sure, you're going be spending the rest of your life with this guy, so won't he cut you some slack right now? Nope. Even the most laid-back guy has needs. As we said before, you can't put your guy on hold because you've got a wedding to plan. He's the reason you're going through all this, remember?

A few weeks before the wedding, and before your stress levels get crazy, think about how you both can avoid turning into raving, bickering lunatics. See if you can lay some ground rules that will prevent unneeded stress before it happens. Look through the list of stress-reducing ideas below and consider hiring a few helpful folks (dog walkers, grocery delivery guys, housecleaners) to get the dust bunnies, dirty clothes, and takeout cartons out from underfoot.

De-stressers:

- During the month before the wedding, hire a weekly cleaning service.
- Get a pet-sitting service to feed, walk, and entertain your pets (especially if you have dogs) for a few days before and after the wedding.
- Find a supermarket or on-line grocery company that delivers. Fill the cabinets and freezer with frozen dinners and quick-fix meals.
- Forget about doing laundry. During the week before the wedding, take everything to a wash-and-fold place.

Scream in the shower, work off your anxiety at the gym, vent to your best friend, but don't take out your craziness on your significant other. Instead, find time to sneak out together and enjoy each other's company. Don't do anything requiring reservations or dressy clothes. See if your favorite bands are playing anywhere in town. Take a stroll through an offbeat part of the city. Get down to the lake, or take a run together around the reservoir. Meet for drinks in an old hangout, or play a game of tennis. Go to a movie and make out in the back row. Go mountain biking, and get sweaty and relaxed. Let yourself have fun with this guy again.

What about the night before the wedding? Traditionally, brides and grooms have spent this night apart. But tradition also assumed that most brides and grooms weren't already living together. If you and your squeeze share an apartment, it can be fun to spend that final night apart. Some brides enjoy the ritual of sleeping one final night in their childhood bed or in their parents' home. Others might opt for a hotel room shared with sisters or cousins, or the guest room (or living-room futon) of a best friend or former roommate. When Stephanie's sister got married, all three sisters squeezed into a room at the Ritz (with Stephanie, the youngest, relegated to a cot, as usual). This was, symbolically, the last time they would all share a room together, so naturally much hysterical giggling ensued, ending only when the bride told everyone to shut up now, she had to get married in the morning. You might want to spend the night alone, to think back over your past and meditate on this step into your new life.

Or this might be the perfect time to connect with your sweetie, lying in bed together and admitting that you're nervous and queasy, that your hands are shaking and your feet are freezing (why do you think they call them "cold feet"?). The two of you can raid the fridge at midnight, eat ice cream at two in the morning, tell all those dumb jokes that only the two of you think are funny, and basically keep each other from freaking out at the enormity of what you're about to do. You decide.

What about the big day? Do you (or does your groom) disappear until you meet down the aisle? Or is he the one helping you into your dress and remembering the bouquet in the fridge? It's entirely up to you. But even the most laid-back guy may get a charge at seeing you suddenly so transformed, and the effect won't be quite as dramatic if he's watched you brushing your teeth and struggling into that body shaper. If you want to get ready in private and you and your sweetie are already living together, don't kick your guy out of the house. Plan to get dressed at your best friend's house or in your sister's hotel room, and designate someone to pick you up in plenty of time. Just give your hair and makeup stylists, and anyone else who might have a legitimately urgent need to reach you, the phone number of where you'll be staying that night, in case of traffic or emergencies.

PUBLIC TIME

Come the day of your wedding, you might feel like there's a loudspeaker in your head blaring Queen's "Under Pressure." You're the center of attention, and everyone wants a piece of you. Arrghhh! First of all, don't assume that you'll get to catch up with all your old friends and far-flung relatives on the day of the wedding. "A wonderful, hectic blur" is how a whole lot of brides describe their weddings—and those were the brides who had fun. If you have a lot of people coming into town, schedule one-on-one times before the wedding. Have tea with your mom; knock back a few Cosmos with your college pals; let your friends at work take you out to lunch.

Once the wedding events begin, you might need a few minutes of cool-off time during the hullabaloo. What to do? Use the classic girls' ploy: head to the ladies' room! Girls *always* go to the bathroom in pairs, and a wedding should be no exception. Grab a pal and head to the nearest mirrored sanctum, especially if it's got comfy flowered chairs and big counters. Sink down in the nearest chair (or prop yourself up against the sink) and indulge in a quick round of gossip. If she's a true friend, she'll even hold up your train while you pee.

What if something goes wrong? Delegate, delegate, delegate. Don't let anyone force you to crack the whip. You're the princess. If something bad happens, ask someone else to run interference for you. Make your mom go yell at the caterer. Let your groom's best man wrestle with the broken microphone. Float like a butterfly, and leave the stinging to those around you.

Remember to think out the post-reception details. Will you be going to a hotel? Leaving for the airport? If you are leaving for your honeymoon immediately after the reception, make sure your suitcases are packed and stashed somewhere safe at the reception site ahead of time. Pack a small bag with your toothbrush, basic toiletries, and traveling clothes and put that

alongside your suitcases. Make arrangements for someone to take home your dress and accessories at the end of the event, and be sure an appropriate bag or box for transporting the dress is stashed with your luggage. If you're going to a hotel after the reception, have someone check your overnight luggage there beforehand. And unless you're planning on getting in the family way immediately, don't forget to toss whatever birth-control method you're using into your luggage, too.

No matter how many hours you spend at yoga class, sometime during the next few months you're going to feel like you're directing air traffic at the world's busiest airport. On Christmas weekend. In a snowstorm. A little advance organization can save you a lot of stress down the line. After all, who wants to spend a whole Saturday morning dumping out every single one of your purses looking for the old bank-machine receipt where you scrawled down the name of that fabulous florist?

Whether your style involves jotting everything down in your Palm Pilot or sticking Post-Its into your journal, creating a master planning guide will save you from wanting to speed-dial Elopements-R-Us two weeks before the wedding. So here are our suggestions for managing your time. Of course, as we've noted elsewhere in the book, not all of you will have the luxury— or the inclination—to spend a whole year getting your wedding together.

This at-a-glance planner should help you figure out your priorities. Feel free to mix, match, and condense as you please. Having a year to get everything done can make your life easier, but you can certainly put together a swell soiree in a lot less time. Getting hitched at City Hall with only your sweetie and your sister? Then nix the part about choosing the bridal party. Need visas for your tropical honeymoon? Jot that down in our handy notes section. Scribble down ideas, staple in swatches, sketch out your dress in eyeliner, make smiley faces in pink glitter ink—whatever it takes to retain your sanity and help you get the wedding you want. Good luck!

The Anti-Bride Timeline

12 months before

Set the date. Check for conflicts with:

Major religious holidays (Not just your own! Do at least a quick skim through the other major faiths that might affect your guests.)

Airline blackout dates.

Horrible weather patterns. Sure, you might be able to get a great deal flying to the Caribbean in September. But do you really want to share your beach with a hurricane? Ditto, say, Buffalo in January.

Set the guest list.

Set a budget.

Decide on the size and style of your wedding.

Choose and reserve ceremony and reception locations.

Choose bridal party and grooms party.

9 months before

Make, design, or shop for invitations. Make sure invitation includes (either on separate cards or all in one): ceremony date, time, and location; reception date, time, and location; map to both; response card; lodging and travel agent/flight information, if appropriate.

Decide if and where to register.

Book a photographer.

Select a florist.

Plan your music. Will you have a harpist or a mariachi band? A DJ or someone hitting the play button on a boom box? Now's the time to start interviewing bands and DJs. If you're putting together your own music, start compiling your songs now.

Research, interview, and hire caterer.

Research, interview, and hire cake baker.

Choose an officiant (or officiants) for your ceremony.

Start looking for your dress.

6 months before

Start writing ceremony.

Keep shopping for dress.

Start planning the décor.

Shop for rings.

Decide on dress for attendants. Basic black for everyone or hand-tailored silk suits? Give
   your attendants plenty of time to get their look together.

4 months before

Compile an address list, and double-check current addresses along with spelling (and
   titles) for all guest names.

Make honeymoon plans. If necessary, get or update passports, get necessary visas.

Start planning the rehearsal dinner (if having).

Buy dress.

2 months before

Find a hotel for out-of-town guests. If you'll be hosting a big posse, you can usually get
   them a group rate at a local hotel, as long as they make their reservations by a
   certain date. Give your guests both a low-frills and a splurge option, and note
   these on the invitations. Then it's up to them to go with your offering or make
   their own arrangements.

Arrange for any alterations.

Get marriage license. Requirements for these vary from state to state, but be sure to allow
   plenty of time for the wheels of bureaucracy to roll your way. You've seen bureaucracy
   in action at the DMV, right? And just like a learner's permit, your license is only good
   for a certain amount of time. So if your wedding gets suddenly postponed, make sure
   to check the expiration date on your license before you say "I do." Some states require
   a medical exam and a blood test, others have pre-wedding waiting periods. Be sure to
   call your local city clerk's office to find out what you'll need to bring with you to get
   your license. And by the way, you both have to be there in person to file the papers.

6 weeks before

Address and mail invitations.

Create a wedding program.

Get a gift for your sweetie.

Schedule manicurist, hairstylist, etc.

Confirm dates, prices, and services with all vendors.

Arrange for transportation of wedding party and guests.

1 week before

Run through details with all vendors.

Confirm any rehearsal and wedding plans with all attendants.

Have the bachelor/bachelorette parties.

Pull together all the elements of your outfit.

Pack for the honeymoon.

Get a facial, dye your hair, get your legs (or anything else!) waxed.

1 day before

Manicure/pedicure.

Massage!!

Don't forget to track down (and pack) the cake knife!

Give your sweetie the present.

The Big Day

Get your hair and/or makeup done.

Have brunch with family or friends.

Relax.

Get married!

Contact List

Officiant(s): _____

Tel: _____ Cel: _____ Fax: _____

Florist: _____

Tel: _____ Cel: _____ Fax: _____

Caterer: _____

Tel: _____ Cel: _____ Fax: _____

Cake Baker: _____

Tel: _____ Cel: _____ Fax: _____

Hotel Manager: _____

Tel: _____ Cel: _____ Fax: _____

Dress Shop or Designer: _____

Tel: _____ Cel: _____ Fax: _____

Hair Stylist: _____

Tel: _____ Cel: _____ Fax: _____

Makeup Artist: _____

Tel: _____ Cel: _____ Fax: _____

Contact List

Photographer

Tel: Cel: Fax:

Videographer:

Tel: Cel: Fax:

Ceremony Space Manager:

Tel: Cel: Fax:

Reception Space Manager:

Tel: Cel: Fax:

Van, Limo, or Car Service Drivers:

Tel: Cel: Fax:

Band leader or DJ:

Tel: Cel: Fax:

Travel Agent:

Tel: Cel: Fax:

Therapist:

Tel: Cel: Fax:

Dress

Dress Size:

Bra Size:

Measurements

Bust:

Waist:

Hip:

Inseam:

Fitting Appointments:

Remember to bring

❏ Dress-appropriate undergarments

❏ Dress-appropriate shoes

Remember to get these in writing: Receipt with amount of deposit, final price
(including price of alterations), date dress will be available, name of salesperson and
store manager, shop's return/reimbursement policy.

Accessories

Veil/headpiece: Style, name of shop or designer, price.

Shoes: Style, name of shop or designer, price.

Coat, shawl, or wrap: Style, name of shop or designer, price.

Undergarments: Style, name of shop or designer, price.

Jewelry

Your ring size:

Your groom's ring size:

Beauty Notes

Your favorite metals, gems, or stones: _____

Name of jewelry store or designer: _____

Depending on how fancy a rock you're getting, it's a pretty good idea to get some insurance on it, just in case you leave it in a hotel soap-dish.

Necklace, bracelet, earrings, other: Style, name of shop or designer, price. _____

Hair

Style sketch

Veil/headpiece: _____

Name of stylist: _____

Rate: _____

Tip: _____

Makeup

Foundation: _____

Powder: _____

Coverup or correctives: _____

Eyeliner: _____

Mascara: _____

Eyeshadow: _____

Cheek color: _____

Highlighter: _____

Lip liner: _____

Lipstick: _____

Gloss: _____

Perfume: _____

Day-of Checklist

Big stuff

- ❏ Dress (well, duh, but you'd be surprised what you can forget)
- ❏ Shoes
- ❏ Lingerie, including bra, panties, stockings, and slip
- ❏ Headgear, including veil
- ❏ Jewelry in a case
- ❏ Scarf or shawl
- ❏ Marriage license
- ❏ Vendor contact list
- ❏ Airplane tickets, if you're leaving for the honeymoon right after the reception

Little Stuff

- ❏ Bobby pins
- ❏ Safety pins
- ❏ Clear nail polish (for stocking runs)
- ❏ Nail polish of the color you're wearing
- ❏ Q-tips
- ❏ Makeup remover (for smudges)
- ❏ Powder compact and lipstick (for during-the-event touchups)
- ❏ Scissors, needle, and thread that matches dress
- ❏ Small travel iron or clothes steamer
- ❏ Aspirin or ibuprofen
- ❏ Straws (so you don't mess up your lipstick)
- ❏ Bottled water
- ❏ Stain remover
- ❏ Tweezers
- ❏ A couple of energy bars, in case you forget to eat
- ❏ Nail file
- ❏ Tissues
- ❏ Band-Aids
- ❏ Toothpaste and toothbrush

Day-of Checklist

❐ Breath mints
❐ Hairspray
❐ Tampons or pads, if needed

Secret Weapons

❐ Duct tape
❐ Safety pins (the tiny gold ones as well a few heavy-duty ones)
❐ More bobby pins
❐ Cell phone
❐ Extension cords
❐ Jumper cables
❐ Cab fare

TIP: *Getting dressed in a hotel room? Make the most of room service. Most big hotels pride themselves on their ability to fill any guest's request, no matter how far fetched. If you run your panty hose or forget your toothbrush, call housekeeping or the front desk. Don't forget to tell them that you're getting married in an hour.*

Overwhelmed? Stunned? At some point during the wedding-planning process, we know you might be tempted to grab your sweetheart and jump on the next plane to Vegas. But before you elope, remember that people love brides. You know how total strangers go out of their way to be nice to you if they find out it's your birthday? Well, no matter what, the thought of a bride—old, young, previously married, blushing, or not—melts even the crankiest heart. So if you lock your wedding dress (and your car keys) inside your truck or you get pulled over for speeding on your way to the ceremony, be shameless about your plight. Tell everyone—the locksmith, the fireman, the police officer—that you're about to get married. Trust us. It works.

Places & Spaces

Area Parks
www.areaparks.com

Get married at a monument!
Castles
www.castles.org
www.castlesontheweb.com
Want to be a princess bride?
Find abbeys and castles a la Paris!

National Park Guide
www.nps.gov
202-208-6843
Unite in nature

Vegas
www.vegas.com
Going to the chapel . . .

Invitations

Big Leap Designs
www.bigleapdesigns.com
Add a little humor to your wedding with these catchy cards

Botanical Paperworks
www.botanicalpaperworks.com
888-727-3755
Natural elements produce fantastic handmade invitations

Cherry Blossom Gardens
www.garden-gifts.com
Design your own invitations with an Asian flair!

Crane's
www.crane.com
They're good enough to make U.S. currency

Marie Versailles
www.marieversailles.com
Original art on fabulous invitations

Papyrus
800-886-6700
Shape your own unconventional invitation

Bridal & Bridesmaids

Amsale
www.amsale.com
800-765-0170
Modern meets traditional

Asian Formal Wear
www.asianformaldresses.com
Asian elegance, just a click away.

Givenchy Bridal
www.givenchy.com
800-341-3467
The bride is sitting pretty with this premier couture

Helen Morley
www.helenmorley.com
Glamour in the big apple

Manale
www.manale.com
Wedding lines with an international flair

Monique Lhuiller
www.moniquelhuiller.com
877-659-9804
Young, sleek, and SEXY!

Nicole Miller
www.nicolemiller.com
A lot more than just little black dresses

Ultimate Bride
312-337-6300
Traditional to trendy bridal attire

Unique Bridal
www.uniquebridal.com
517-662-7458
Truly unique, with tons of designers

Vera Wang
www.verawang.com
212-628-3400
Quintessential bridal collection

Vintage Clothing & Accessories

Amy Pang
www.amypang.com
310-729-2240
Asian glamour with a vintage twist

Anthropologie
www.anthropologie.com
Vintage-style jewelry and accessories

Davenport & Co.
www.davenportandco.com
Fabulous wedding gown collection from every fashion era

Decades Inc.
www.decadesinc.com
323-655-0223
Easy request forms for savvy brides

eBay
www.ebay.com
The thrill of the hunt: find those 1920s flapper bridesmaids' dresses

Enoki World
www.enokiworld.com
314-725-0735
Incredible Japanese vintage

Fashion Dig
www.fashiondig.com
'Ask Janet' will find you those mysterious vintage Vera scarves

Julie Slinger Work Room
415.673.6788
Custom handbags and ring pillows

Keni Valenti Couture
www.kenivalenti.com
212-967-7147
Retro designer couture

Paper Bag Princess
www.paperbagp.com
310-358-1985
Look like a celebrity at your wedding

Piece Unique
www.pieceunique.com
310-444-0452
Modern and retro couture united

Popula
www.popula.com
Find that old Gloria Gaynor record or 1950s cocktail dress here

Rusty Zipper
www.rustyzipper.com
The bride and groom can find everything from belts to cufflinks

Vintage Vixen
www.vintagevixen.com
941-351-7956
Hello, glamour! Spectacular '50s collection

What Comes Around Goes Around
www.nyvintage.com
212-343-9303
Groovy Emilio Pucci collection; international suppliers

Discount Bridal

A Classy Touch Wedding
www.aclassytouchwedding.com
336-288-3283
An inexpensive route to glamour

Advantage Bridal
www.advantagebridal.com
(877) WED-SHOP
Check out the checklist that would make mom proud

Discount Bridal Services
www.discountbidalservice.com
800-874-8794
Fabulous online consumer guide!

Netbride
www.netbride.com
1-800-GO GOWNS
Create your own veil and get instant quotes

Savvy Bridal
www.savvybridal.com
805-527-9111
Shabby chic

Jewelry

American Gem Society
www.ags.org
800-346-8485
Experts will tell you how to choose your gems

Ashford Jewelry
www.ashford.com
888-922-9039
These jewels will steal your heart, again

DeBeers Jewelers
www.adiamondisforever.com
Find out why those ads are so fabulous!

Fantasy Jewels
www.fantasyjewels.com
410-435-5599
Funky vintage costume jewelry

Forbeadin'
415-641-1414
Fabulous custom-beaded earrings, necklaces, tiaras

Hellmuth Simply Good Fine Jewelry
800-744-5586
Classic rings and jewels even your mother will like

Indulge
www.indulge.com
800-463-8543
Indulge your bridesmaids with cool bracelets, scents, or scarves

Jaffe Jewelers
www.thering.com
800-THE RING
Timeless elegance and modern grace

Links of London
www.linksoflondon.com
877-79LINKS
Unique jewels from across the pond

Mondera Jewelry
www.mondera.com
800-MONDERA
Eternal creations for over 100 years

M. Schon
www.mschon.com
*Hello, Mod Squad—totally modern jewels
for the bride or groom*

Riviera Costume Jewelry
800-221-4854
*Accessorize with style; for you and your
bridesmaids*

Robert Lee Morris
www.robertleemorris.com
212-431-9405
Trendy meets traditional

Roule Jewelry
www.roule.com
212-475-9329
*Feel the love with this ultra-cool Braille
jewelry*

Sage Jewelry
www.sagejewelry.com
877-698-SAGE
*Vintage necklaces, rings, and tiaras; plus
custom blended scents*

Van Peterson Jewelry
www.vanpeterson.com
888-826-7383
Exotic designs from around the world

Zales Jewelry
www.jewelry.com
800-311-5393
*Brilliant collection of diamonds
and other gems*

Makeup

BeneFit Cosmetics
www.benefitcosmetics.com
800-781-2336
Oh, la la! Cutting edge cosmetics.

Clinique
www.clinique.com
Natural beauty? Try this Web site.

Heather Kleinman's
Cosmetic Connection
www.cosmeticconnection.com
Tips, make overs, AND shopping

Lancome
www.lancome.com
Straight from Paris, international beauty.

The Body Shop
www.the-body-shop.com
*Beauty products that are green and good
for you!*

Registry

Barneys New York
www.barneys.com
THE premier in The Big Apple

Crate & Barrel
www.crateandbarrel.com
Fashion for your home

WeddingChannel.com
www.weddingchannel.com
Tons of different places to register in one place

Tiffany & Co.
www.tiffany.com
The crème de la crème for the bride and groom

Target
www.target.com
Who doesn't love Target?

Williams-Sonoma
www.williams-sonoma.com
Gorgeous housewares

Men's Resources

Brookes Brothers
www.brookesbrothers.com
800-274-1815
From suits to three-piece tuxes, this is a classic choice for him

George D. Anthony
www.georgedanthony.com
800-786-9902
Fabulous men's couture, from vests to cummerbunds

Gingiss Formal Wear
www.gingiss.com
Fabulous men's fashion

Keswani & Sons
www.keswani.com
800-255-7267
This tailor will construct the groom's own design, anywhere

Marrying Man
www.marryingman.com
Everything the groom needs to know for the big day

President Tuxedo
www.prestux.com
800-TUXEDO1
Hello, James Bond!

The Kilt Store
www.thekiltstore.com
44-0800-018-5458
Finally, find out what they wear underneath their kilts!

Tuxedo World
www.tuxedoworld.com
Hundreds of hot tuxes

General Resource Web sites

www.bridalplanner.com
Read up on your wedding with their selection of books

www.ibride.com
Fresh tips of the day, everyday!

www.marthastewart.com
Of course . . . Martha!

www.theknot.com
The hottest wedding Web site

www.weddingbells.com
Where every bride is an anti-bride

www.weddingchannel.com
The resource locator on this site is fabulous!

www.weddingcircle.com
Funky ethnic wedding resources

www.weddingguide.co.uk
Give a little British flavour to your wedding

www.weddingnetwork.com
Great advice for the modern bride

www.weddingromance.com
Totally interactive live chats, so you can talk all you want about weddings

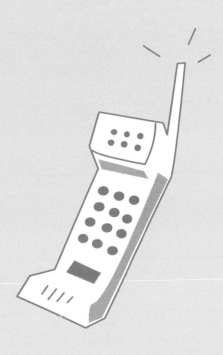

Says Carolyn:

For Laurent. My best friend, inspiration, and surf instructor; eloping with you and having our wedding on 2 coastlines, 3 cities, and 2 countries was the most exciting and liberating experience of my life. To our parents, Pat, Barry, Agnes, and Jean, who didn't pressure us to go the traditional route and understand our spirit. To the fabulously talented gals (and one boy) who made this book happen: Wyndie Nusbaum, the best dress maker and friend a girl could ever have; Iris Hough, style by the truckload, and my soul sister for 20 years; Julie Slinger, designer extraordinaire, your friendship, talent, and wisdom, are priceless; Sage Machado you are as sparkling as your jewels; Jean Danielson of BeneFit Cosmetics, great ideas, great products; Donna Davis, you are a jewelry genius; and Johnny Thompson, no one knows "do's and don'ts" better than you. To the bartenders of 26 Mix and the Cassanova for making the magic margaritas that made those interviews flow. To Beth Loudenberg and Donnie Norwood, for your friendship, and loyalty. To my sisters, Joan and Kathy, for understanding why there was no bouquet to catch. To the true anti-brides and grooms: Iris and John Hough, Chris Hall and Alison Rothman, Julie Slinger and Gary Huckaby, Juli Shore and Stephen Sonke, Kristin Spence and Colin Berry, Gina Bartlett and Eric Halpern, Niall and Jeannie McCallum, Gino and Carola, and Mike and Ellen Harris. To Jennifer Dhillon for being in my corner 24-7. To Mikyla Bruder, our editor, for fighting for a good idea, and making it a better one; and Sara Schneider, our design director, for protecting and improving our vision; To Abby Featherstone, our star researcher; to Stephanie Rosenbaum for saving the day. To Dwight Eschliman, who knows how to "not shoot" a wedding and make it gorgeous. To Danique Zimmerman for your excellent eye, judgement, and willingness to pitch in wherever needed; to Bert Green for building our book right from cover to cover; and finally, special thanks to Ithinand (Bird) Tubkam, for your dedication, friendship, all those long nights, outstanding professionalism, and continually striving for design and illustration excellence 365 days a year.

Says Stephanie:

For my sisters, Michele and Amy, for playing the Bride Game with me all those years. To Eric, for laughing at all the right places, and for Ruby! To Paige Rogers, for great bride advice, invaluable friendship, and much-needed rounds of gimlets at the Lex. Loads of rice and kisses to all the real-life brides, grooms, and long-suffering bridesmaids who shared their stories for this book. Special thanks to Molly and Davina, Paige and Rob, Michael Slass and Renee Roub, Sarah Kennedy Kline, Christy and Victor Stabin, Katrina Hendriks, Jill and Owen, Lisa and Brent LaMotte, Leslie Jonath, Brian Bouldrey, and the always fabulous and inspirational Christina Vickory, Shar Rednour, and Jackie Strano. Many thanks to Elizabeth Faulkner for her very helpful assistance on the cake section. And especially to our editor, Mikyla Bruder, for her endless patience, good humor, and talent.